HOMER

1. *Silver coin from Ios with head of Homer, fourth century* B.C.

HOMER

C. M. Bowra

DUCKWORTH

First published in 1972 by
Gerald Duckworth & Company Limited
43 Gloucester Crescent, London NW1

ISBN 0 7156 0616 6

Printed in Great Britain by
Western Printing Services Ltd, Bristol

Contents

	List of Plates	vii
	Foreword	ix
1	Introduction	1
2	Oral Composition	10
3	Obstacles and Difficulties	32
4	Devices of Composition	54
5	The Greek Heroic Age	79
6	The Iliad: its Shape and Character	97
7	The Odyssey: its Shape and Character	117
8	The Poetry of Action	141
9	The Creative Outlook	165
	Bibliographical Note	183
	Index	185
	Acknowledgments	192

List of Plates

Frontispiece

1. Head of Homer

Between pages 6 and 7

2. Linear B tablet from Pylos
3. Stirrup jar from Eleusis
4. Alphabetic script on Attic Geometric jug
5. Rhapsode

Between pages 22 and 23

6. Young soldiers arming
7. North-eastern corner of the citadel, Troy VI

Between pages 38 and 39

8. Horse skeletons in a Salamis tomb
9, 10, 11. Three versions of the blinding of Polyphemus

Between pages 46 and 47

12. Bronze helmet from the Warrior's Tomb, Knossos
13. Boars' tooth helmet
14. Ivory plaque of a Delos warrior
15. 'The Warrior Vase'
16. The Rhodian plate
17. Hoplite armour from Argos

Between pages 54 and 55

18. Lion Hunt dagger from Mycenae

19. Gold and silver pin from Mycenae
20. 'Nestor's cup'

Between pages 86 and 87

21. A house in Troy VIIa
22. The 'Great Casemate' at Tiryns
23. Gold funeral mask from Mycenae
24. Vaphio cup II
25. Gold diadem from Mycenae

Between pages 102 and 103

26. Briseis and Phoenix
27. Hector and Andromache
28. Achilles and Patroclus
29. Funeral games of Patroclus
30. Achilles and Hector fighting
31, 32. The ransom of Hector

Between pages 134 and 135

33. Coin showing the monster Scylla
34. Odysseus' companion escaping under a ram
35. Penelope and Telemachus
36. Odysseus and the Suitors

Between pages 150 and 151

37. The great hearth, Nestor's palace, Pylos
38. A bathroom at Nestor's palace, Pylos
39. Ithaca

Foreword

AFTER Sir Maurice Bowra's death on 4 July, 1971, nine chapters of this book were discovered among his papers. The first five chapters were evidently ready for the printer. Chapters 6–9 were not quite ready to go to the typist for their final copying, but when they were inspected it became clear that very little remained to be done to them. It may be that before finally dispatching them to the typist their author would have made some changes. But I am sure that these changes would have been very small; and all I have done to these chapters is to correct typing errors.

The last chapter was to have been called 'Summary and Survival'. Its absence is a matter for great regret. But we have thought it better not to add a chapter with this heading from another hand, but to print Bowra's book as he wrote it. It is hoped that the series will include a book about the history of the Homeric poems from the time of Homer to the present day, and that should in some measure serve as a substitute for the missing chapter.

Christ Church, Oxford   HUGH LLOYD-JONES
5 September, 1971

CHAPTER ONE

Introduction

By common agreement European literature starts with two long poems, the *Iliad* and the *Odyssey*, which the Greeks attributed to Homer. Though they seem to have been composed on the western sea-coast of Asia Minor, their remoter ancestry was on the Greek mainland, and they are European in their character and their posterity. They have had an incalculable influence not only on the subsequent literature of Greece, but also on that of Rome and on much of mediaeval and modern Europe. This comes from the sheer quality of their poetry, which has enthralled succeeding generations, no matter how different their backgrounds and their outlooks. The Homeric poems possess in a very high degree the qualities which we regard as essential to great poetry, and any lover of it responds to them. Yet the very strength of their impact provokes questions, and if we wish to understand their art, their aim and their spirit, we have to know how they were composed, in what social and what literary circumstances, and we must be prepared to find that these are in some ways alien to us and easily misjudged. We must try to see the poems in their own setting and to grasp why they show such characteristics. If we can answer some of these questions, we shall be better qualified to appreciate the poems as works of art.

Though for us the *Iliad* and the *Odyssey* stand in isolated splendour and have no predecessors, there is no reason to think that they sprang fully formed from the Greek genius. They are clearly the product of a long process of which we know nothing because it flourished before the return of writing to Greece after a gap of over four hundred years and therefore left its poems unrecorded. In recent years small scraps of poetry have been found incised on pots, and if they are correctly dated to the years just before or just after 700 B.C., they may be more or less contemporary with the Homeric poems. Since they come from places so diverse as Athens, Ithaca and Ischia, they show that the committal of verses to writing was already widely diffused at this date, though the introduction of the Greek alphabet cannot have been much earlier than 750 B.C. But the argument for a long past behind the Homeric poems comes from the poems themselves. At every point they betray the influence of a powerful tradition. From it come the metre, the stylised, complex language, the literary devices such as similes, the names of the chief personalities, the outline of the main episodes, the frequent use of speeches, the repeated lines which keep the story going, the standard epithets for persons and places and things, the unwillingness of the poets to state their own views or to pass judgments on the action. The poems use this technique and this material with a confident command. To the poet or poets we owe the highly personal impression which the poems make, but they themselves rise from an art which was fully mature when it reached this form. Of any preceding poems we know nothing, but we can recover some of their characteristics and even their contents by detecting what is manifestly traditional in the Homeric texts.

By common convention the *Iliad* and the *Odyssey* are called epics, and this is justified by the Greek word *epos* which amongst other duties is applied also to them. At the least it means that they are long narratives in verse, distinguished by a detachment and a dignity not shared by all such narratives. The appeal of this attribution is that it classes the Homeric poems with other long poems which resemble them in scale or temper or subject, notably with some famous works which try to rival them, such as Virgil's *Aeneid* or Camoens' *Lusiads* or even Milton's *Paradise Lost*. Yet this is where the classification breaks down. For these other epics are conscious imitations; their manner is not spontaneous like Homer's, nor are their stories told simply for their own sake; they abound, as Homer does not, in secondary and symbolical meanings. In the end the use of the word 'epic' for the *Iliad* and the *Odyssey* brings as much confusion as light. Nor need the Homeric poets have confined their art to long poems. It is clear that short poems were equally familiar, and these should come under the same heading. We must look elsewhere if we wish to classify the Homeric poems with precision.

This enquiry calls for an application of the comparative method. If we can find other poems like the *Iliad* and the *Odyssey*, we may hope to understand them better. But the danger with this method is that it unlocks too many doors, and any use of it calls for a strict and cautious discrimination. It has long been recognized that the Homeric poems have something in common with the Anglo-Saxon *Beowulf* and the Norman-French *Song of Roland*, and, somewhat differently, with the various versions, in at least six languages, of the old Semitic and pre-Semitic *Gilgamesh*. The scale of these poems is about a quarter of the Homeric, but they resemble the *Iliad* and the *Odyssey* in their assessment of human worth and of the events which test it. They are heroic, as the Homeric poems are, and this is their leading characteristic. They tell of men and doings greater and grander than in the poet's own generation, and of struggles and efforts which at times transcend human powers. If such poems are primarily heroic, this fixes their main character, and the question of scale is of secondary importance; for a large number of heroic poems, from those of the Norse *Elder Edda* and the Anglo-Saxon *Maldon* to recent pieces recorded from Slavonic peoples, are short, often very short indeed. Even when, exceptionally, they are long, their manner and their method tend to be those of short lays extended to a large field. We know enough about some of them and about their origin and production to suggest possible parallels in Homer. If we can make sure of these, we can postulate circumstances for Homeric authorship which are very different from those in which modern books are written and read. Through these differences we may hope to explain some Homeric characteristics.

Comparative study comes into its own when, in dealing with works of an unfamiliar kind, we find that our own standards and assumptions are irrelevant. We need parallels to illumine what happens outside our own experience and to show how what may seem impossible to us is in its own conditions natural and necessary. It is never easy to find the right, complete and exact parallel, and if we choose the wrong one, we may be led far astray. Homeric criticism presents many salutary lessons, and though there are countless manifestations of it, they fall into recognizable main groups. Behind many lie similar assumptions and a similar uneasiness or discontent with the poems as we have them. The so-called analytical views of Homer arise from these and agree in postulating the existence of more than one author for each poem. In antiquity no such theories existed, but in 1664 Francois Hédelin, Abbé d'Aubignac, tried to demonstrate that the *Iliad* fell short of classical ideals of composition because it was full of contradictions, omissions, loose forecasts or unfulfilled intentions, and the like, and advanced the theory that it was a collection of separate poems, not necessarily or even probably by the same poet, which had been put together in the sixth century B.C. in a clumsy mechanical way. The Abbé was a pioneer of the new criticism, but his work, which was not published until 1715, after his death, made its first real impact in 1795 when Friedrich August Wolf took it up, strengthened it with new arguments and a much more robust scholarship, and gave it to the world in his *Prolegomena ad Homerum*. Where Wolf led, many others have followed. Their approaches fall roughly into three main kinds.

First, it has been argued that the *Iliad* and the *Odyssey* are compilations of separate lays from different hands, and this accounts for the inconsistencies, inequalities, and contradictions which have been detected in them. This was the view of Karl Lachmann, who thought that the same thing had happened to the Middle High German *Nibelungenlied*, and though he was wrong in this, he might have claimed a more recent parallel when he published his theories in 1837–41. In 1835 Elias Lönnrot had published the first edition of the *Kalevala*, which he had put together from a number of separate Finnish lays and, though he made no secret of what he had done, claimed that the result was in some sense the national epic of Finland. It is highly unlikely that the lays, which vary enormously in content, temper and worth, were once parts of a single whole, and though Lönnrot excised some passages and added others of his own making, the result is not a unified poem. In 1857 the same thing was done for Esthonian traditional lays by F. R. Kreutzwald in the *Kalewipoeg*, which followed Lönnrot's methods and produced a similarly haphazard compilation. In more recent times the same thing has happened in Armenia, where many lays from different hands have been woven into a long poem, *David of Sassoun*. It betrays the multiplicity of its origins at every turn, but is still regarded in some romantic or mystical sense as a national poem, even though it is the work of many poets. It is easy to understand why Lachmann believed that some Greek Lönnrot had compiled the Homeric poems and why other scholars took up the idea in revised forms. Yet the theory in all its shapes is based on a false analogy and wrong assumptions. There is no need to think that the Homeric poems are shapeless, haphazard compilations, or that they show anything like the variations of matter and manner so visible in the Finnish, Esthonian and Armenian constructions.

A second view, which at least got rid of the incompetent editor as the source of trouble, was that the poems were expanded, altered and interpolated over the years, and were what is called 'traditional books', like parts of the Old Testament. A parallel was found in the vast Indian epics, the *Mahābhārata* and the *Ramayana*, which seem to have begun as truly heroic narratives but to have had huge tracts of theological and other material inserted into them. It was comforting to think that this happened to the Homeric poems, and critical scholars, who seldom agreed with one another, thought that they could detect interpolations from the disturbance which they brought to the narrative. But here too the parallel was delusive. The large tracts of interpolated matter in the Indian epics are not narrative but theological and instructional, just as they are in the Old Testament. This was natural enough in societies in which a ruling caste of warriors gave place to one of priests, who took over traditional poems and reshaped them to

suit their own outlook. But this is not at all the case with the *Iliad*
and the *Odyssey*. The alleged interpolations are on a par with the
rest of the narrative and resemble it in all respects. If they were
added by later hands we have to explain why, and no explanation
is forthcoming. The alleged parallel is authentic but its application
to Homer is too inexact to be useful.

A third view, which had some vogue in the first years of this
century, was that the poems were put together from existing
poems but not at random. Some respectable poet took poems
already existing but added his own passages to them and shaped
the result to a single design. In this the *Nibelungenlied* was again
quoted as a parallel, with more justification than by Lachmann;
for it has considerable internal confusions and yet is in some sense
a whole. It was thought that the *Iliad* and the *Odyssey* incorporated other poems round a central core, which was in the first
poem the wrath of Achilles, and in the second the vengeance of
Odysseus on the Suitors. This theory has the advantage that it
allows a certain shape and construction to the poems. In a powerful form it was advanced in 1916 for the *Iliad* by U. von Wilamo-
witz-Moellendorff. He thought that differences of manner and
outlook in various parts of the poem indicated differences of
authorship, but he recognized that a guiding hand had been at
work, even if he thought that the end of the *Iliad*, which had once
been brutal and bloodthirsty, had been lost and its place taken by
Book xxiv. This theory presupposes the existence and more or less
common use of writing; for without it no bard could annex large
parts of other poems for his own use. Yet we may doubt whether
writing was used on anything like this scale when the poems were
composed, and if it was not, the theory falls when it postulates
exact boundaries between original and appropriated work.

These three types of theory, with their many variations, indicate
the range of views held by scholars in the last two hundred years.
They have one point in common—they insist that the Homeric
poems were not composed like an ordinary modern narrative.
The poems are thought to be somehow abnormal and to call for
special explanations. They are in many ways so strange to us and

2, 3, 4. *Many of Homer's archaic forms of speech are foreshadowed in Linear B syllabic script, in use in Mycenaean Greece from approximately 1400 to 1200 B.C.* ABOVE: *a Linear B tablet from Pylos.* BELOW LEFT: *an inscribed stirrup jar from Eleusis. After some 400 years, alphabetic writing first appeared.* BELOW RIGHT: *an inscription on an eighth-century jug—a prize in a dancing contest—'He who performs best shall have me'.*

violate so much that we take for granted that scholars resort to far-flung speculations. They agree that the poems cannot have come into existence in a straightforward way like a modern book, and in their uneasiness they offer explanations in the hope that parallels may be found to justify them. But even the most seductive parallels have flaws, and in the end none of these views meets the full needs of the situation. It is just conceivable that a series or group of poets was able to maintain the high poetical level of the *Iliad* and the *Odyssey*, but it is not conceivable that they composed the poems in any of these ways.

Against the Analysts are arranged the so-called Unitarians, who believe that both poems are the work of a single author or at least that each poem is. This is *prima facie* permissible. The Greeks themselves attributed both poems to Homer, and though some cranks at Alexandria believed in two separate authors, one for each poem (Seneca, *On the Brevity of Life* 13), none believed in a number of them. The poems have a sustained manner which is naturally explained as the personal style of a single poet. It is easy to read them without noticing the inconsistencies which disturb the critics. The Unitarians argue that what matters is the actual poetry, the worth of the words, and in this they see a creative, individual touch, which is ignored only by those who are deaf to poetry. They assert that great poets are rare at any time, even in ancient Greece, and that, though the Analysts claim to see grada-tions of worth in different parts of the poems, the standard is on the whole wonderfully sustained. If Homer sometimes nods, that is after all to be expected, and it is remarkable that he so seldom does. It is idle to argue that if the Greeks could produce three tragedians of highest merit in the fifth century, they could have produced as many or more epic poets at an earlier date. The tragedians differ from each other enormously, but the alleged epic poets are strangely similar, and that makes all the difference. It is unlikely that a number of poets should compose so well over so large a field. The Unitarians may be regarded as mugwumps by the Analysts, but they in turn regard the Analysts as Philistines. In the last resort the Unitarians assert that even obvious flaws in the

5 *A rhapsode recounts one of the two great epic poems. From an amphora of the fifth century B.C., when such professional narrators were a feature of the major festivals.*

poems must be accepted because the poet follows his own rules and is not subject to alien standards; so any questions about his behaviour involve a *petitio principii* and are ruled out.

At first this may sound convincing. After all, we expect poets to go their own way, but this way need not be unintelligible. We may reasonably ask why at times the poet falls into what looks like obvious faults, and if we find no answer, we feel that there is something wrong, that not the poet's creative personality is to blame but circumstances over which he has incomplete control. It is hard to believe that a poet so good as Homer is unaware of matters to which we attach importance, notably in the structure of narrative, whether short or long. If he is partially unaware, then the explanation must lie in circumstances unfamiliar to us but familiar to him. In asking why he composes as he does, we find the Unitarian doctrine as inadequate as the alleged parallels of the Analysts. What right have we to think that so good a poet as Homer was unaware of points which mean a lot to us? Was he not also an artist in words, eager to make the most of them? And if he was, would he tolerate awkward breaks and obstacles in his narrative or moments when it is not clear what he means to say? It is not enough to argue that he was a primitive poet, for he is outside any scheme of ancient or modern, primitive or advanced. Though the anomalies of manner do not prove multiple author-ship in any strict sense, they must prove something, and the refusal of the Unitarians to consider them is a denial of reasonable argument. If multiple authorship seems to fly in the face of reality by its insistence on a number of similarly gifted poets, the Uni-tarian dogma is no better, for it refuses to recognize that, though every poet follows his own rules, there must still be an explanation for what look like very peculiar oddities.

It seems then that each of the two main lines of Homeric criticism leads to a dead end. The reason is that, while we try to explain Homer by modern methods of composition, he worked in quite a different way which imposed a special character on his poetry. In recent years comparative study has tried to explain this by adducing closer parallels than were available in the nineteenth century. Yet there remains much to explain, and there is always a danger that a parallel which elucidates one problem will fail with another. If we are convinced that we have found something truly illuminating, we may press it as far as we like; though we shall not get answers to all our questions, we are likely to shape them in a more intelligent spirit. The problem of Homeric authorship has caused trouble for three hundred years, and its final solution still eludes us. In the meanwhile we must remember that even this problem, fascinating though it is, is important only because it helps us to understand the poems and start with a fresh mind in reading them. We may even avoid the temptation to condemn this or that passage not on its merits but because of some theory which claims that it is not authentic.

CHAPTER TWO

Oral Composition

IN considering the nature of Homeric poetry our primary evidence comes from those passages in the poems which tell of bards and their manner of performance. In the *Iliad* Achilles in his tent sings of 'the glorious doings of men' and accompanies himself on the lyre (ix 189–91). In the *Odyssey* there are professional bards, Demodocus at the court of Alcinous in Phaeacia and Phemius at the court of Odysseus in Ithaca. They are not princes or nobles but free men who rank with craftsmen, such as seers, physicians and workers in wood (17.353), and depend on princely patronage for a living. We do not know of what Achilles sings, but the professional bards sing of recent events, Demodocus of a quarrel between Odysseus and Achilles (8.73–82) and of the Wooden Horse (8.500–20), and Phemius of the return of the Achaeans from Troy (1.325–7). The songs are very short, and Demodocus sings at least two in an evening. Homer says nothing at all about composition on a large scale like that of the *Iliad* and the *Odyssey*, and suggests that short lays were what he knew. Nor is this the only respect in which his imaginary bards fail to conform to his own practice. They sing of the immediate past, and though this may give pain to Penelope, Telemachus explains: 'Men applaud more that song which is the latest to float round the ears of men' (1.351–2). Homer himself sets his events in a dateless past, when men were stronger and braver than in his own day. So though he may be assumed to record contemporary practice in singing lays, it is not entirely his own way.

Homer certainly throws light on his notion of composition. He says nothing about bards learning their art from predecessors;

he does not even agree with Hesiod that Memory is the mother of the Muses (*Theogony* 60). He suggests something different. When Phemius, who has been forced to sing to the Suitors, begs Odysseus to spare his life, he says:

'I am self-taught, but a god set in my heart paths of song of every kind; I am fit to sing before you as before a god.' (22.347–9)

Phemius claims first that he has taught himself, and second that he is inspired by a god. The two claims are not incompatible, especially if he means that he has never had a human master in his art but has relied upon a god to guide him, and taken full advantage of what he gives. This claim to inspiration agrees with what is said elsewhere. We are told that a god has bestowed the gift of song on Demodocus (8.44), and Odysseus implies this when he praises him for his performance:

'Either the Muse, daughter of Zeus, or Apollo, has taught you.' (8.488)

Alcinous has already said of the bard:

'On him the god bestowed song in abundance, to give delight in whatever direction his heart stirs him to sing.' (8.44–5)

and that Homer shared this view is clear from his invocation to the Muse to sing at the start of the *Iliad* and the *Odyssey*.

This inspiration is not haphazard. What Phemius gets from a god is 'paths of song of every kind', and this means that he knows all the tricks of the trade, not merely all kinds of theme but all the ways to deal with them. That is why he is able to accede at once to the request of Odysseus for a song about the Wooden Horse (8.500 ff.). When Odysseus praises his earlier singing for being 'in order' (8.489) and hopes that his next song will be 'duly performed' (8.496), he means much the same for both, that the song tells of historical events as they should be told. Homer recognizes that heroic song has its own standards and that care for truth is among them. In all this a high degree of craftsmanship is implied, and the respect for it comes out when, after Odysseus has told his own long story, Alcinous congratulates him by saying 'you have told your tale with knowledge like a bard' (11.368). What the god gives is shaped and tempered by the poet's own judgment and experience, and this is very much the view held by later Greek poets such as Pindar. Homer gives to his imaginary bards a view of poetry which looks like his own, and we surmise that they reflect his own training and methods.

Homer's bards sing to a listening audience; they do not write books for readers. Writing is mentioned once in the *Iliad* (vi 168–9) in the story of Bellerophon, and then it has the air of being something mysterious and rare, an echo from a far past, not fully understood. Though Homer may have known of writing, he did not think it proper to introduce it into a heroic story, except as a dark element in a remote legend. It is not mentioned in the *Odyssey*. The Homeric poems, like the lays which they describe, are products of an oral art, composed for, and directed to, listeners who do not read. Such an art precedes written poetry and has an enormous vogue in illiterate and semi-literate societies. In the latter class it often survives when writing is confined to legal and religious documents. If the Homeric poems may be classified generally as oral, they may be classified more specifically as oral heroic. Such poetry is nearly always lost after performance, but very occasionally it is written down, as indeed the Homeric poems were at some stage of their career. There are elsewhere other stray survivals from what was once a very widely spread art in many parts of the world, and these specimens may be supplemented by modern texts taken from recent recitations. In Europe these are still available, or were until recently, in parts of Russia, Jugoslavia, Albania, Greece, and Bulgaria; in Asia especially among the Turkic and Mongol peoples of the USSR, the Ainu of Hokkaido, the Malays of Borneo, the Achins of Sumatra. In Europe the art is moribund, and though it is kept alive artificially, it lacks authority and authenticity; in many parts of Asia it still maintains an indigenous strength. It has no standard form, and its themes vary from the wildest fancies to popular history. A poem of this kind may be wholly or partially memorised, and repeated performances give it a certain continuity, but this lasts only so long as its own special circumstances. If these change, it may disappear, unless by some whim or chance it is recorded in writing. This is very exceptional, and we cannot begin to imagine how much oral poetry has been lost for ever.

Oral heroic poetry, as we now know it, is entirely relevant to the study of Homer. In his bards he indicates that he was familiar with a form of it, even if this was not in all ways what he himself practised. One of his bards, Demodocus, varies his tales of human events with a tale of the gods, when he sings of Ares and Aphrodite (8.266–366), and this association of tales of gods with tales of men is found in the *Elder Edda*, while divine dealings with men inform much of *Gilgamesh*. Gods and goddesses, spirits and angels, demons and devils abound in other heroic poetry, and may be assumed to be normal to it. Even when it is ready to pass beyond them and to concentrate on purely human actions, it finds it difficult to dispense with them, as the *Song of Roland* marks the hero's death with a supernatural darkness and the flight of angels. The Homeric poems give a substantial place to the gods and their dealings with men, and in heroic poetry this is not exceptional.

When Homer indicates that songs of glorious doings were meant to be heard, he must be taken seriously, since before the invention or the diffusion of writing this must have been the sole manner of poetical performance. This has long been recognized in the case of Homer, but its full consequences were not drawn until some forty years ago a young American scholar, Milman Parry, started a new line of enquiry which produced results[1] so fruitful that he has been called 'the Darwin of Homeric studies'.[2] Parry began by a systematic study of repeated phrases or formulae in Homer and examined especially the noun-adjective combinations for gods and heroes. He dealt also, but with less precision, with other recurring phrases, with repeated single lines, and with repeated blocks of lines, which he called 'themes'. He argued that these formulaic elements had been worked out with great care and

[1] These may now be studied in Milman Parry, *The Making of Homeric Verse*, Oxford, 1971.
[2] H. T. Wade-Gery, *The Poet of the Iliad*, Cambridge, 1952, p. 38.

economy and fashioned not merely for oral performance but even for improvisation or extemporary recitation. The formulae meet almost every demand of composition, and if a bard is master of them, he can face any situation that his story demands.

The implications and the consequences of this theory are endless, but first we must see how it works. *1.* The noun-adjective combinations are needed alike for proper names of gods, heroes, peoples and places, for natural phenomena and all kinds of man-made objects, and indeed for anything concrete that is expressed by a noun. The given noun is not always accompanied by the same adjective, but the noun-adjective combination varies with (*a*) the grammatical case, (*b*) its place in the verse, and (*c*) the space occupied by the combination in the verse. Thus Achilles has no less than twenty-four epithets, but each is determined by one or more of the above needs. *2.* Recurring phrases take up part of the line and do not obtrude themselves on our attention. They could in fact occur in a language much less formulaic than Homer's, but of course if the bard knew them he would welcome them for use. The first ten lines of the *Iliad* contain at least ten such minor formulae, and the first ten lines of the *Odyssey* thirteen. *3.* The single repeated line is a valuable resource in poems of action where certain events are constantly recurring, the coming of dawn and dusk, the death of warriors in battle, the throwing of spears, a man walking with his dogs, the clasping of one man's hand by another, a warrior leaping from his chariot to the ground, the triple invocation of Zeus, Athene and Apollo, washing and oiling the body, seating a guest on a chair, and indeed all the unobtrusive machinery needed to make a narrative solid and real. *4.* Longer passages or themes are used for similar purposes, like getting chariots ready, putting a ship to sea or bringing it to land, the conduct of a sacrifice or a feast, a warrior arming, stabling and unstabling horses, activities of wild and domestic animals, and phases of day and night. Their function resembles that of the single lines, but they are more prominent and attract more attention.

Parry's argument, which an early death prevented him from developing to the full, was that the formulae of Homeric poetry represent a very highly developed art, fashioned for recitation and ready to meet any requirement in it. The bard's task was to use the material at his disposal as well as possible, so that he would not be caught at a disadvantage if asked suddenly to sing on a new theme, as Demodocus is asked by Odysseus to sing about the Wooden Horse (8.500–20). Parry worked out with great care that part of his theory which dealt with noun-adjective combinations, especially those concerning persons. In these the adjectives are not particularized or intended to have any weight or precision of meaning. Such meaning as they have soon becomes dimmed with repetition, and we cease to pay attention to them. They are primarily functional and meant to help composition. They are beyond question the creation of a long tradition of active bards, for no single bard or generation of bards could have evolved so elaborate a system to meet all foreseeable needs in so remarkable a way. Parry's insistence on their relevance to Homeric art is entirely right, but it is only part of a more embracing conception which he would have developed if he had lived longer.

The wide range and high adaptability of Homeric formulae is partly due to the metre which they serve. The hexameter, like other Greek metres, works on the quantitative system which was normal in the older kinds of Indo-European verse, but its form is specifically and uniquely Greek. Between its invention and its Homeric employment enough time passed for an enormous armoury of formulae to be fashioned for it. Just because the metre is complex, formulae must be far more varied than in the simple metres of most oral poetry. For instance, the lax Russian metre can accommodate almost anything, and the Jugoslav, consisting of five trochees, is not difficult to manage, nor always managed with skill. But when a difficult metre like the hexameter is combined with a highly inflected language like Greek, the formulae must be varied to satisfy the many different requirements of metre and syntax. Indeed Greek heroic poetry seems unique in the obstacles which it presents to extemporary recitation, and this means that the bard must be richly equipped with formulae to meet every challenge.

Once a suitable formula has been found to meet a certain combination of needs there is no necessity to have another to meet precisely the same needs, even though it may have a slightly different sense. On the whole the Homeric formulae are fashioned with economy, but there are certain variants, whose significance is not easy to assess. First, there are sometimes alternatives to the usual noun-adjective combinations. These have the same case, the same scansion, and the same place in the line as the commoner forms, and are in themselves quite simple. In the two poems Odysseus is 'of many wiles' 81 times, but 'sacker of cities' 4; Zeus is 'cloud-gatherer' 30 times and 'lightning-gatherer' once; Hera is 'white-armed' 3 times and 'golden-throned' once; Apollo is 'son of Zeus' twice and 'famed with the bow' once. All these characters have other epithets to suit other needs, but these genuine, if unnecessary, doublets indicate that the conventions governing formulae were not absolutely hard and fast. Nor is much gained by these occasional alternatives, which soon strike us as purely mechanical. A possible exception is when Zeus is called 'lightning-gatherer' (xvi 298), for he is said to be moving clouds and it would be clumsy to call him by the usual title of 'cloud-gatherer'. This does not prove much, but at least it indicates that the poet was aware of his formulae and able under pressure to vary them.

Secondly, there is some variation in the standard recurring lines. Thus the coming of a new day is commonly introduced by 'when early-born, rosy-fingered Dawn appeared', which occurs 22 times, but there are occasional alternatives to it, and these are themselves not standardized, notably the paratactic 'the sun struck afresh the fields' (vii 421; 19.433), or 'Dawn, in her saffron robe, spread over all the world' (viii 1), or 'Dawn rose from the bed of glorious Tithonus that she might bring light to immortals and mortals' (xi 1; 5.1). It is not clear why these variants are used. Perhaps they are meant to mark a rather special occasion at its start; perhaps they indicate a desire to break away from a formula which has become too standardized. More striking is the variety of phrases which mark the death of a warrior in battle. A common form is 'Down he fell with a crash and his armour rang upon him', which occurs seven times, but the rival 'Dark death and mighty fate took him' occurs three times. Moreover there are several alternatives even to these, as for instance the first half of a repeated line occurs seven times in the form 'Down he fell with a crash', but the second half deals with a different topic. Much more striking are the occasions when the fall of a hero is marked by a simile, notably with Asius (xiii 389–91) and with Sarpedon (xvi 482–4) who are treated with the same words:

He fell as an oak falls or a tall pine, which craftsmen carve with newly-sharpened axes to be a ship's timber.

Death is so common on the Homeric battlefield that more than one formula is needed to save it from monotony, and we may assume that in these variations the poet knew what he was doing.

These variations make it clear that the Homeric style is rather less ossified than some critics claim or than modern parallels in Jugoslav and Russian undeniably are. It looks as if in Homer's time the style, though already ancient and traditional and fully formed, could still admit and absorb new elements and was not compelled always to repeat the same formula for the same purpose. We can even see to some degree how new formulae were shaped, and though some of these may be earlier than Homer and the process may well be ancient, the manner of formation is important. The practice is to reshape an existing formula so that a new formula emerges. The vital need is that the new formula should have the same metrical value as the old and some similarity of sound, but not necessarily of sense. We cannot always tell which is the old and which the new, and sometimes we must assume that both are derived from a third which we do not possess. There is a close affinity of sound between the words used about a sacrifice of oxen, 'and the sweet savour of the fat came all about me' (12.369) and Odysseus' comment when he hears the cry of Nausicaa's women, 'the womanly cry has come about me' (6.122). The similarity is almost entirely of metre and sound, and hardly at all of sense. The same is true of *piona dēmon*, 'fat soil' (14.329) and *piona demōi*, 'rich with fat' (9.464), or between the twang of Odysseus' bow, 'like a swallow in its sound', (*audēn*) (21.411) and Athene 'like a swallow to look at', (*antēn*) (22.240). In such cases we surmise that in feeling for a phrase to express an idea the poet is guided by his huge store of existing phrases and so maintains the unity of the poetical style. This reaches very deep into the language of both poems, and the units which betray such creative imitations are nearly always short and therefore easily assimilated. One phrase suggests another, and the process of creating new phrases keeps the language alive.

Once a formula had been found and absorbed, it could be used endlessly. but we can only guess why certain formulae were preferred to others. It is, for instance, notable that many epithets in the noun-adjective combinations are used commonly with different names and are not in themselves at all distinguished. For instance the word *dīos*, which means 'noble', is attached to a number of heroes, both famous and obscure. It may be of ancient origin and come from the early days of heroic song when it sought to emphasize the greatness of its characters rather than any particularities. Metrically it is indispensable, and that is the reason why it stays. But few epithets are so colourless as this. Even in some of the most stock formulae the epithet must have been chosen in the first place for some appeal in it. The formulae are often of a striking distinction and cannot have been fashioned or selected casually. We suspect that some struggle for existence has taken place, and the best have survived. It is only because they occur so often that we cease to notice and admire them. The epithets for things, whether natural or man-made, are much more than distinguishing labels—'rosy-fingered Dawn'; the sea 'loudly resounding' or 'wine-dark' or 'unharvested'; 'honey-sweet' fruit; willows that 'lose their leaves'; the sky 'brazen' or 'starry'; lions 'bred on the mountains' or 'baleful-hearted'; death 'that lays at length'; ships 'well-benched' or 'well-balanced' or 'with scarlet cheeks'; 'long-shadowing spear'; 'silver-studded sword'; shield 'like a tower'. Of course not all epithets are so lively, and we must accept 'dark night' and 'bright moon' and 'bright sunlight', but though these are not dazzling, they are apt and truthful. When we first read Homer, we are struck by the liveliness of the epithets, and later, when we know the epithets of other oral poets, we mark their inferiority both in quantity and in quality. In fashioning their machinery for recitation generations of Greek bards attended to the smallest details. Constant repetition might in the end dull the audience's interest, but at least at the start the epithets had an attraction which justified their place in a poetical style.

The same perceptive skill could hardly be expected in epithets for persons or peoples or places or even gods. Yet some of the leading persons are credited with well-defined characteristics, which belong to tradition and account for their epithets. For instance, Odysseus was known both for his cunning and for his endurance. So three of his standard epithets refer to the first, and three to the second. He is also, no doubt for metrical convenience, called 'noble', but only three times. Achilles was renowned for his fleetness of foot, and two of his most frequent epithets refer to this. But he was also a formidable warrior and is called 'breaker of men' and 'lion-hearted', but the first only three times and the second only once. Evidently 'swift-footed' was thought right for him and ousted most other claimants. Agamemnon, as commander-in-chief of the Achaean forces at Troy, has six epithets, each with a different metrical worth, referring to it. Otherwise he is 'famous' or 'godlike' or 'huge', but no epithet conveys any marked personal trait. Conversely, Penelope, who needs all her cunning to keep the Suitors at bay, is called 'of many gifts', but otherwise 'sensible' and 'prudent'. Her role is fixed by the legend and the poet keeps it. Sometimes an epithet seems to come from a lost past. Nestor has several rather conventional epithets, but he is also 'the Gerenian knight', and this may be connected with Geren in Messenia, the seat of some of his youthful exploits. Otherwise most characters have epithets which can easily be transferred from one to another and do not in themselves throw much light on the persons to whom they are attached. Their use is to give the bard a split second of time while he recites, and thereby to ease a little his concentration of effort.

On the other hand the peoples whom Homer names are treated

with some care. In the epithets for them a well-informed tradition is at work. Even quite minor peoples like the Carians and the Lycians are not neglected, the first being 'barbarous-tongued' (ii 867; x 428), and the second 'shielded' (xvi 490, 541, 593), both of which are historically correct. They indicate that in finding epithets for peoples Greek poetry aimed at something distinctive. This of course was combined with other aims. The Greeks who besieged Troy are called by three names in Homer—Achaeans, Danaans, and Argives. The first is historically correct, since it occurs in Hittite documents of the fourteenth and thirteenth centuries. The second may be equally correct, since it occurs, though more rarely, in Egyptian documents of an even earlier date. The third seems to come from a time when the whole Peloponnese was known as Argos, and this would be before the Dorian invasion of *c.* 1100. The three names survive because each has a different scansion, nor are the epithets for Danaans and Argives very illuminating, since the first are 'warriors', 'servants of Ares', 'strong', 'with swift horses', 'lovers of war', and the second 'warriors' and 'lovers of war'. But twice (iv 285; xii 354) the Argives are called 'bronze-shirted'. No doubt this comes from their association with Achaeans, who are given this epithet 28 times. Its interest is that it reflects an historical state of affairs, when the Achaeans actually wore bronze body-armour. The same state of affairs is reflected in the other epithet 'well-greaved' with the less common metrical variant 'bronze-greaved'. This is true of the Greeks in the fourteenth and thirteenth centuries but not between about 1200 and the eighth century. Greaves were, it seems, a uniquely Greek accoutrement, and called for emphatic notice.

The Trojans are also treated with some regard to historical fact. They are called Dardanians, and this must come from the district of Dardania where Troy lies. As such their only epithet is 'fighters hand to hand', which says nothing special. More interestingly, though the Trojans have twelve different epithets which stress their prowess in war, they are also called 'trainers of horses' 21 times, while the same epithet is given to their commander Hector.

This is founded on fact. The cities VI and VII at Hisarlik, which correspond to the Homeric Troy, are rich in horses' bones, and there is no doubt that the Trojans bred horses on their rich plain, which was in the first years of this century the breeding-ground for the stud-farm of the Sultan Abdul Hamid II. This epithet is as true for the Trojans as 'well-greaved' for the Achaeans. Both must go back to a very early date, when they were deserved by their distinguishing correctness.

In dealing with places it was obviously convenient to have certain epithets which would be right almost anywhere, such as 'goodly', 'well-built', 'beloved', 'holy'. But sometimes a real knowledge is displayed and confers a special prominence. The ruins of Tiryns show that it deserves 'walled'; Pylos, with its enclosed bay, is certainly 'sandy'; excavation has proved that Mycenae amply justifies 'rich in gold'; Lacedaemon, under the mass of Taygetus, is aptly 'hollow'; Egyptian Thebes, outside Greek experience, is 'hundred-gated'; Boeotian Thebes, 'seven-gated', accords with legend; Dodona is 'stormy'; Calydon is 'rocky'. These epithets are right enough in their contexts and show personal knowledge or sound information. One or two others, which receive greater prominence in the narrative, indicate a more special acquaintance. First, Ithaca, on which so much of the *Odyssey* takes place, has seven epithets, which is not extravagant in view of its importance. Of these 'sea-girt', 'rocky', 'craggy', 'rough' all fit what we know of it. 'Clear' is true enough on most days, and the unusual 'under Neïos'—the local mountain —looks right. When it is called a 'rich soil' (14.329), we doubt whether the poet really knew it, but on the whole his information, as reflected in his epithets, is not far from accurate. Troy presents a more interesting case. It shares with other cities such epithets as 'lovely', 'well built' and 'holy', and these do not mean very much. Much more distinctive are 'steep', 'with good horses', 'well-walled', 'with good towers', 'beetling', 'windy', 'with lofty gates', 'wide-streeted', all of which have been justified by the excavation of the site and show that the tradition was well informed on the look of Troy from without and within.

In finding epithets for gods a different problem arose. The bards were restricted to such as suited a god's functions and character. We might expect Homer to use cult-titles or titles connected with shrines, but he seldom does so. When Apollo is asked to stop the plague, he is called 'Mouse-god' because mice spread plague (i 39), and when Achilles makes libation before sending Patroclus to battle, he calls upon Zeus, 'lord of Dodona, Pelasgian, dwelling afar' (xvi 233). The first adjective recalls the connexion of Zeus with the oracular shrine of Dodona; the second may refer to his bonds with the legendary first inhabitants of Greece, but is hardly a cult-title. This is about as far as such titles go. But some of the epithets are certainly ancient. One or two defy interpretation. When Hermes is called by a word translated 'fast traveller', we know its meaning not from ancient scholars but because part of the word was current in the archaic dialect of Arcadia and meant 'hurry'. Stranger but not inexplicable are the adjectives given respectively to Hera and Athene and translated conventionally 'soft-eyed' and 'bright-eyed'. Literally, they mean 'cow-faced' and 'owl-faced' and must come from a time when goddesses had features or characteristics of animals or birds. The same probably explains why Apollo is called 'wolf-born' (iv 101). He seems once to have been a wolf or had some of a wolf's qualities. Homer disregards this and places the epithet with another, 'famed with the bow'. It survives because it is ancient.

Apart from these few special cases, which are old and honoured, most epithets of gods are pictorial or descriptive, and in them a discriminating fancy is at work. Aphrodite is sometimes 'golden', sometimes 'laughter-loving'. Poseidon is 'holder of earth' and 'shaker of earth'—the latter as god of earthquakes. He is also 'blue-haired', which suits the Greek sea. Zeus has some 39 epithets, which stress variously his position as king of the gods, father of gods and men, lord of the thunder and the lightning, guardian of suppliants, seated on high on Olympus or Ida, the greatest and most powerful of the gods. Between them they complete the picture of Zeus as the sky-god who rules heaven and earth. Though we soon cease to notice these epithets, they have

6. *Greek soldiers don corslet, helmet and greaves on this Attic kylix of the fifth century* B.C. *The characteristic bronze greaves were a distinctive part of Achaean armour in the fourteenth and thirteenth centuries (see pp. 20, 47)*

done their work at the start by making us look at the gods in a
certain way. There is no doubt about the preeminence of Zeus or
the allurements of Aphrodite. Even Thetis, the sea-nymph and
mother of Achilles, makes an unforgettable impression as 'silver-
footed', while the divine smith Hephaestus, who is lame from
childhood, has an adjective which means literally 'with both feet
crooked'. It seems wasteful to coin such epithets and then to let
them fade away through too much exploitation, but that is what
happens. If they hardly affect the actual narrative, they still do
something to catch the minds of audiences and to accustom them,
almost unconsciously, to this unified heroic world.

Though considerable care must have been given to the selection
of epithets for the poet's repertory, the same care is not found in
their use. Because their first task is to suit metre and syntax,
precision of meaning is often neglected. Often enough they say
nothing relevant; sometimes they are contradictory or discordant.
We are surprised when the Cyclops is called 'god-like' (1.70) or
'great-hearted' (10.200), or the mother of the beggar Irus 'lady
mother' (18.5), or the herdsman Philoetius 'leader of men' (20.185),
or the blackguard Aegisthus 'blameless' (1.29). There are some
obvious misfits as when by day the sky is 'starry' (viii 46; xv 371;
9.527), or beached ships 'swift' (x 306; xi 666; xvi 168), or dirty
linen 'shining' (6.26). Yet there are moments when the poet seems
more conscious of his epithets and gives them a new edge. First,
he sometimes makes full use of them so that they enhance the
sense, as when Achilles leaps forward against Apollo, 'Three
times then did swift-footed, godlike Achilles leap forward' (xx 445)
or in the battle with the river-god Scamander, 'whenever swift-
footed godlike Achilles leapt to stand against him' (xxi 265).
Secondly, there are moments when we expect a conventional
epithet, and get instead something different. When Circe realises
who Odysseus is, she uses not the epithet usual in this place, 'dear
to Zeus' but 'of many wiles' (10.330). Though after a masculine
caesura Odysseus is normally 'famed with the spear', he is twice
called 'Ithacan' (2.246; 22.45), which may stress his position as the
only man who can restore order in Ithaca. When Achilles prepares

7. *The far-distant Troy of Homer is a 'great city', 'well-walled' with
'good towers'—a description justified by the excavations of Troy VI and
VIIa (see pp. 21, 81).*

the funeral rites of Patroclus, he is not 'swift-footed' but 'great-hearted', as though this were more appropriate to his behaviour on this solemn occasion (xxiii 168). Thirdly, there are other moments when the conventional epithet seems to convey an ironical intention. When Achilles sits in his tent, he is still 'swift-footed' (i 489), but that could mark the contrast between his normal state and his present inactivity. When he defiles the streams of Scamander with blood, the river-god complains, 'My beautiful streams are full of corpses' (xxi 218), and normal and abnormal are contrasted. When Helen speaks to Priam about her brothers who are absent from Troy, she does not know that they are dead, and the poet comments, 'But them already the life-giving earth covered there in Lacadaemon, in their own native land' (iii 243–4). The 'life-giving earth' is a formula, but here it has a noble pathos. The epithets are occasionally varied or used beyond their strict purpose. This does not amount to very much, but it accords with the other liberties which a bard could enjoy inside his conventions.

The abundance of formulaic phrases was taken by Parry to prove that the language of Homer was intended for recitation, and that recitation implies some degree of extemporary composition. Having worked this out in theory he then tested it in the field, and examined the actual practice of oral heroic bards in Jugoslavia, who use formulae on a very large scale. Their tradition goes back to the fourteenth century and deals with the 'glorious doings of men'. Though the songs are usually short, bards, if given sufficient warning and encouragement, and intervals to recuperate, are able to compose long poems, even as much as 12,000 lines, which is the length of the *Odyssey*. The formulae resemble the Homeric in falling into four main categories, and an occasional misfit of epithets is noticeable, as when the Moors have 'white' hands. The Jugoslavs at times incorporate new themes such as telephones and aeroplanes, and in this respect resemble Homer when he introduces an innovation such as the Gorgon's head on the shield of Agamemnon (xi 36–7) or the sheaths in the brooch of Odysseus (19.226–31). These experiments are made by adapting existing formulae. Since the Jugoslav art is entirely oral and depends not at all on writing, it is a legitimate surmise that Homer's was the same.

On the other hand, the parallel between Jugoslav and Homeric practice is not absolute, and the divergences call for attention. First, the Homeric poems are richer than the Jugoslav in every respect. The episodes are more various; the similes are more numerous and more detailed; the language is more abundant and more flexible. We guess that Homer's is an aristocratic art, meant for princes who kept bards for their entertainment, rather as they are kept in the *Odyssey*. The Jugoslav songs belong to a lower level of society, above which is a higher, literate level which pays no attention to them; the Homeric songs speak for a whole society in which everyone is known to everyone else. The greater richness of the Homeric language encourages a nobler and finer poetry. The Jugoslavs have vigour and grandeur, but Homer has both on a more generous scale and very much else besides. Secondly, Homer uses many more formulae and many more variations on set themes than the Jugoslavs, and this is forced on him by the elaborate nature of his metre. The Jugoslav trochaic pentameter is easy to compose, and suits the emphatic accent of the language with its propensity to an accent on the penultimate syllable of a word. The Greek metre compels the creation of variants, so that it may include the different cases of the noun and its different places in the line. For Jugoslav these problems hardly exist.

The greatest difference between the Jugoslav and the Homeric poems is one of quality. Lively and forceful though the former often are, they very seldom attain the Homeric amplitude and humanity. Of course this is inevitably due to the rarity of poetical genius, and it is entirely possible that in the past Jugoslav bards were better than any of those known to us. But something also must be due to the lower social level at which the Jugoslavs work. In this matter closer parallels may be found in the oral epics of central Asia, notably those of Turkic and Tatar peoples. These illuminate the Homeric poems in ways that the Jugoslavs do not.

First, they attain at times really fantastic lengths, longer than the *Iliad* and the *Odyssey* combined. Two Kirghiz bards, Saghimbai Orozbakov (1867–1930) and Saiakbai Karalaev (born in 1894), have each produced their own version of *Manas* and each is of about 250,000 lines. Poems of such length would probably not have been composed but for external prompting from literary scholars, nor would we be able to assess their worth and contents but for the aid given by writing, tape-recording, and printing, but at least they show that it is possible for an oral poet to compose on a very large scale. Secondly, these poems have a remarkable range of temper and effect and are delightfully inventive and conscious of the variegated human scene. Thirdly, they are directed to whole societies, in which there may indeed be different levels, but all levels enjoy long performances of heroic song. They too reveal their dependence on tradition in the use of formulae, but though these do not reach the Homeric richness, they are more varied than the Jugoslav.

The Homeric language is rich, not only in possessing a large number of formulae but in having acquired them from many sources. It was never, and never could have been, a spoken language. It is a language created for poetry, especially for the hexameter, with its demanding metrical needs. Such a language was needed if the poems were to be understood in more than one place, and in Greece it was almost an international language which had to be learned by performers and their audiences but, because it drew on many sources, had vast opportunities for rich and various effects. Its variety comes partly from its appropriation of words and forms from different stages and areas of Greek. If in general it has the external appearance of the Ionic dialect spoken on the west coast of Asia Minor, it also shows traces of Aeolic, spoken further north on the same coast. We do not know how or when such elements came into it, but their presence indicates that the epic grew to maturity in Asia Minor. Behind this are many other words which seem to be older and drawn from a different source, notably some which in historical times were current only in Arcadia or in Cyprus or in both. These are survivals from the

Mycenaean language spoken in the Peloponnese before the Dorian invasion and then isolated in the mountains of Arcadia and the remote island of Cyprus, which received Mycenaean refugees or colonists in the thirteenth century. In the Homeric poems these words, and no doubt others which cannot be so well certified, seem to have come from Mycenaean times, and indicate that even then heroic song was in existence.

The origins of the poems are lost, but it is quite conceivable that songs of the Trojan War began actually during it or soon after it, and then passed into a more general repertory. Gradually the special, poetical language was built up from various sources, not merely from different dialects, but from the artificial adaptation of existing forms to suit metrical demands. The poems abound in synonyms, alternative forms, syllables lengthened or shortened to fit the hexameter, words misunderstood even in early times and never fully explained. There are five forms of the infinitive 'to be' and of the imperfect 'was'; the archaic w at the beginning of some words is neglected or observed as it suits the poet's need; two vowels in collocation are sometimes contracted, sometimes not; some participles and infinitives are given an additional internal vowel to bring them into the verse; the syllable e, prefixed to verbs to denote the past tense, is often omitted; the first foot of the hexameter is not always a pure dactyl or a pure spondee but forcibly assumed to be one or the other. The Homeric language is a truly artificial creation, shaped over a long period, and though much of the formation must have come in Ionia after the Greek colonization of $c.$ 1100, it may have begun earlier on the mainland, and the deciding factor throughout was the need to enrich and strengthen the hexameter. There may have been local varieties of heroic song, but the dominating style was what we know as Homeric.

We have said that this language was evolved for recitation, but this calls for clarification. Recitation may involve a degree of improvization, and the improvizing poet must rely on his command of formulae already fashioned. Such improvization is quite common, but when a poet operates only with familiar formulae, the chances are that his performance may not be of a very high quality; for the personal element and the individual touch will always add something, and their absence keeps the song at too conventional a level. This is specially noticeable when the bard is called upon to sing of some subject which has no regular place in his repertory or which he may be attempting for the first time. When the great Russian scholar Radlov asked a Kirghiz bard to sing on an unfamiliar theme, he was able to do so, but the result was feeble and uninteresting. In the first years of Parry's discoveries it was sometimes assumed that the Homeric poems consisted entirely of formulae, and that, however much we shrink from the idea, we must endure it. But this is not necessary, nor even likely. First, we cannot be certain that a set of words is formulaic unless it occurs more than once, and in the Homeric poems a great many sets occur only once. Secondly, though a poet may learn a large number of formulae, there is no reason why he should not invent others, especially when he has something unusual to say. Though he performs orally, he is capable of shaping large parts of his poem in his head as his own creation, and though he uses formulae and creates other phrases to match them, much of his work is not formulaic. Thirdly, the formulaic style is created not to be a complete means of expression for every conceivable theme or situation but to provide a structure on which a more personal means of expression can be built. This was evidently the case with the poems of the *Elder Edda*, *Beowulf* and the Assyrian version of *Gilgamesh*, all of which contain a substantial proportion of formulae but also much else that is not formulaic.

Homer has a larger element of formulae than these, but he seems to have operated in much the same way, by combining existing formulae with fresh inventions. In general these poets told of characters and episodes that had often been told of, but they added something of their own, not merely in their interpretation of events but by advancing beyond formulae to free composition. Since the poet did not rely upon written texts and had not been brought up on reading, his memory would have to be very good

and enable him to shape in advance what he intended to say. If by
chance he faltered or forgot, he could at a pinch improvise enough
to keep going for a while. When we consider the marvellous richness of the Homeric poems and the embracing scope of their
poetry, it is easier to believe that they were the work of a bard or
bards who not only knew all the tricks of the tradition but could
advance it by coining new phrases and new effects and perform
with consummate ability because they had thought it out before-
hand. This hypothesis at least helps to explain how Homer
maintains so high a quality and is in this respect rare indeed among
known oral poets.

This helps also to counter a doubt which has troubled some
scholars. Some devoted admirers of Homer have felt that this
reduction of poetry to a series of formulae deprived the poems of
their claim to be creative works of art. What had been thought to
be divine inventions of his fancy were shown to be no more than
mechanical devices to help recitation. It was not realized that these
mechanical devices might still be beautiful, or that an age-old
machinery need not have been fashioned by uninspired hacks. Yet,
even if the poems consisted of nothing but formulae, they would
not for that reason be worthless. A literate poet composes with
single words which he chooses for their individual worth to him,
and we judge him by his choice and combination of them. A
formulaic poet composes with formulae, and it is by his choice and
combination of them that he is judged. A new combination of old
formulae may lead to an entirely unforeseen result; many formulae
change their tone with the context, and something new may
always emerge. Formulae may be used with creative effect, and
this is what Homer does. The oral poet is likely to make his
supplements conform to the existing formulaic manner and to
model new phrases on old. So the tone is maintained and the poetry
does not lag or sag.

The Homeric style is beautifully straightforward and easy to
follow, and this is largely because it is formulaic. The fundamental
formulae often consist of half-lines, which may be combined with
others equally short to achieve a joint result, and these results are

for this very reason easy to grasp. We know the parts, and the sum of them presents no difficulty. Moreover, because the short phrase is ultimately the primary unit of composition, sentences are usually short, and more often than not end with the end of a line. Even when a word is carried over to the next line, it is not very important and tends usually to amplify what is already clear. Long sentences are rare; paragraphs are made of simple units. The speed and the lightness of Homeric poetry, so alien to the deeply meditated and associative language of Virgil, come from the formulae, and particularly from their being so well concentrated and polished by time and use. There is nothing otiose in them, and their meaning is immediately clear. This clarity is a great source of strength, and though Homer seldom gives us lines to ponder as we unravel their cloudy complexities, yet he again and again gives lines which for their sheer simplicity and strength, their immediacy of attack and surety of aim, go far beyond most literate poets. This manner suits his matter, and is part of his triumph.

Homer's vocabulary and his use of it were largely an inheritance from the past, from a long succession of bards who passed on their art and its technique from generation to generation. His own imaginary singers may claim that they are self-taught or owe everything to the Muse, but the Muse is the embodiment of what they have learned, as well as of the creative spirit which sets them to work. This is true not merely of literary devices. The words, formulaic or not, embody a mass of material, of stories and characters, of everything necessary to a heroic tale, and these could either be kept intact or altered to suit the poet's intention. From the analogy of other oral poems we know that such changes are extensive over the years, that heroes who were separated by centuries, are brought together in the same event, that ancient folk-tales about animals are transferred to human beings, that alternative versions of a single story grow apart and become quite different, that even hallowed stories may be changed in the interest of novelty or some revolution in opinion. Though the examination of formulae is important, it is part of the wider study of the Homeric poems as the products of a long tradition, which seems to have had its roots in the Mycenaean age and reached its apogee in the second half of the eighth century B.C. Inside this tradition, at this high moment, the individual poet had a part to play, and it is our task to inquire how he played it.

CHAPTER THREE

Obstacles and Difficulties

BECAUSE the Homeric poems were composed for recitation, some of their characteristics are alien to us who are brought up on books, and these have been misjudged and made the basis of elaborate theories of authorship. The most noticed and indeed the most noticeable is the prevalence of apparent contradictions in the narrative. These are of two main kinds. First are those occasions when a later passage seems to say the opposite of what has already been said, sometimes by neglect of an obvious passage, sometimes by giving a different emphasis and direction. Second are actual omissions, which we find hard to accept since we are not accustomed to silence on actions which we think indispensable to a coherent narrative. We expect a clear flow of events and are troubled when we have to supply connections on which the poet says nothing.

We may begin with a notorious triviality, if only to get it out of the way. Too much notice has been taken of it but it none the less illustrates a principle. An entirely unimportant person, Pylaemenes, king of the Paphlagonians, is killed by Menelaus (v 576), but considerably later appears as a mourner at his son's funeral (xiii 658). To this there is a parallel in Ariosto's *Orlando Furioso*, where Ballustrio is killed (16.45) but later takes a busy part in the action (40.73; 41.6). Ours might be an occasion when, as Horace says (*A.P.* 359), Homer nods, and nobody need think the worse of him for it. If mistakes of this kind occur in written texts, which a poet can control, they are much more likely to occur in oral recitations over which his control is weaker. However, in this case it is possible that Homer was misled by his reliance on formulae.

When Pylaemenes mourns his son, his name, mentioned earlier, is not repeated, and all we hear is 'and with them went his father shedding tears' (xiii 658). This cannot be proved to be formulaic, since it occurs only here, but it looks a conventional part of the apparatus of mourning. If it is in place here, it may be allowed to introduce a small contradiction. Equally unimportant is the paradox that Agamemnon's sword is at one point 'silver-studded' (ii 45), whereas at another 'gold studs shone upon it' (xi 29–30). At the first place Homer uses a standard epithet for a sword, and no doubt it came more or less automatically; at the second he is describing with some care the armour of Agamemnon before he sets out for battle, and this calls for distinctive attention. The contradiction is natural and does not matter in the least. Again, an omission, which amounts to a contradiction, can be explained on the same lines. When Athene comes to Ithaca in the form of Mentes, she enters the palace and puts her spear against a pillar in a spear-stand (1.127–8). This is what guests do, and it excites no interest. Later, when she leaves, she takes the shape of a bird and flies away, and the spear is forgotten. It is of no significance and there is no need to explain it away.

The audience of an oral poet has no books of which it can turn back the pages to recall what has been told earlier. Once something is said, it leaves no record except in the memory. The reciting bard has to impress what he says on his hearers and make it clear and firm; otherwise their minds will wander, and his performance will fail. He is forced to concentrate on his main themes and give to them every care; he must select what really matters and omit anything that delays or obstructs his movement or detracts from his main intention and his central effects. His rule is 'one thing at a time', and this governs his narrative. If on the one hand it accounts for certain gaps which we may find a little worrying, on the other it helps to explain his beautiful clarity. If the gaps were filled they would hinder the direct development, and that is why they exist. Exception has been taken to these omissions, but if we look at them we see how trivial most of them are.

When Poseidon comes to the battlefield, we hear about his golden chariot and his horses with golden manes, whom he tethers with golden shackles (xiii 23 ff.). The glittering description strikes a fresh note and is well suited to a god. But when he leaves the field, nothing is said about the horses (xv 218). Repetition would be tedious, and there is no need to pick up the theme. Homer wishes to get the god off the scene and to start a new episode, which he does with speed and economy. So too when Athene and Hera come to help the Achaeans, their preparations are described in full (v 711–52), as befits a pair of goddesses driving to the battlefield. But when they have played their part, and the poet moves to a new theme, we hear no more than that they go back to the house of Zeus (v 907). In the confusion of battle such a technique is even more necessary, if we are to mark properly what matters. When Achilles cleaves his way through the Trojans, he lays down his spear by a tamarisk, and keeps only his sword (xxi 17), but soon afterwards (xxi 67) he has his spear in his hand, though we do not hear that he has picked it up. Again, when Hector meditates on his forthcoming encounter with Achilles, he rests his shield against the wall of Troy (xxii 97), and we are not told that he takes it up, though he has it a few minutes later (xxii 111). In these cases a simple action is reported, either as part of the story or for some attractive element in it, but there is no need to resume it later at the cost of distraction from the main theme.

The call to say one thing at a time and to keep it free from inessential additions affects more important actions than these. It may not matter if heroes like Agamemnon, Diomedes, and Odysseus get seriously wounded but recover almost at once; it is part of their heroic nature that their wounds heal quickly, and the centre of interest has shifted to another phase in their careers. More illuminating is the case of Diomedes, who says to Glaucus:

'If you are one of the immortals who have come down from the sky, I would not fight with the gods who live in the sky.' (vi 128–9)

We are surprised to hear Diomedes saying this, since in the preceding book he has fought against and wounded both Aphrodite (v 330 ff.) and Ares (v 855 ff.). We are not told why he has changed his mind, and we have to infer his motives from the action. At this point it takes a new turn. Whereas before Diomedes was able to distinguish gods from men because Athene had given him the power to do so (v 127–32), now this power has evidently left him. It has served its purpose, and that is the end of it. It gives a special character to the actions of Book V; in Book VI Diomedes' career follows a new direction, and the old power is no longer his. Homer follows his rule of concentrating on a single point and disregarding anything that interferes with it. Something of the same kind happens on a more extended scale when Odysseus has his shape and appearance changed by Athene into that of an old beggar (13.429). The change is complete, in clothes, limbs and strength, and its purpose is that he may not be recognized when he comes to his home for the destruction of the Suitors. It works very well. To make him known to Telemachus Athene restores his old appearance but only for a few moments, and then he is once again a beggar (16.172). To repeat the process again would be tedious and distracting, and Homer gets round it. The moment comes when Odysseus prepares to fight the beggar Irus, who has insulted him, and the poet tells what happens:

Odysseus girt his rags about his privy parts, and revealed his thighs, beautiful and strong, and his broad shoulders were revealed, and his chest, and powerful arms. (18.67–9)

It is clear that Odysseus is already in possession of his old strength, as he proceeds at once to show at the expense of Irus. A little later when the old Nurse Euryclea washes his feet, she notices his likeness in body and voice and feet to the Odysseus whom she knew twenty years before (19.380–1). When she recognizes him by the scar on his foot, this merely confirms her suspicions. Odysseus is not said to be brought back to his first splendour; he gradually regains it and we do not need to be told explicitly of each stage in this recovery.

This concentration on the dramatic present explains why the poet sets certain high occasions where we do not expect them and where they might seem to contradict something in the narrative. But this is done on purpose. For instance, the scene between Hector and Andromache (vi 370 ff.) is not only complete and wonderful in itself but performs the functions of a farewell-scene between them, for it looks as if it were their last meeting. Nor indeed are they brought together in this way again in the poem. We may perhaps assume that it is placed comparatively early to avoid any need for repeating it when our attention must be turned to other matters with which it might interfere. Yet if we press the details of the text, husband and wife do meet again; for at vii 310 the Trojans go back to Troy, and we must assume that Hector spends the night with Andromache. The poet does not say so, and it may be stupid to think of it. What matters is that by placing the scene between husband and wife relatively early in the poem Homer is free to develop to the full Hector's heroic qualities in battle. A similar technique is used for the parting of Odysseus from Calypso. When Calypso knows that he must leave her, she addresses a moving speech to him, and he replies with graceful and grateful courtesy (5.203 ff.). In fact he does not leave her till the fourth day after this, and in the interval they see each other and sleep together as before (5.225–7), but there is no further converse of words. Here too one thing is done at a time. The farewell has to be got out of the way before the poet gets on to the absorbing business of Odysseus building his raft. This has a different intention and a different temper, and must be kept separate.

The concentration on the moment becomes more urgent when an action is spread over more than one book or begun at one point, left halfway and then taken up again later. The poet must not disturb his new developments by harking back to what has happened before. When Achilles has refused the overtures of Agamemnon in Book ix, it is surprising to find him saying a little later:

'Now I think that the Achaeans will take their place around my knees in entreaty; for a need comes on them that they can endure no longer.'

(xi 609–10)

We must not conclude from this that Book ix is a later addition and that this passage knows nothing of it. Homer focuses his attention on the moment, and when he makes Achilles speak like this, it is because he wishes to stress how little the offers of Agamemnon have touched him. Now as Achilles sees with his own eyes the extent of the Achaean disaster, he is fully aware that his prayer has been answered and that the Achaeans are indeed being defeated without him. This is the present point, and it sharpens Achilles' desire, now fully awake, to humiliate Agamemnon. A little later, when Achilles yields to Patroclus' entreaties to join the battle, he speaks only of the present. His opinion is that the Trojans would be easily routed 'if lord Agamemnon had had kindly thoughts towards me' (xvi 72–3). Achilles still does not treat Agamemnon's overtures seriously and puts him entirely in the wrong. At this crucial moment when he is about to send Patroclus to war, he still holds that the dark situation would never have arisen if Agamemnon had behaved properly. The offers made do not yet appease his sense of grievance, and in this speech he begins to yield by letting Patroclus go to battle. His wrath is still at work in him but there are signs that it will not last in its present form for much longer. Achilles is indeed taking the first steps which will lead him to paying for it.

A special source of trouble, spread over several books, is the wall of the Achaean camp. The alleged difficulties are: (*a*) at vii 435 the building of the wall is described, but at xiv 31 it seems to have been built at the beginning of the war; (*b*) at xii 10–33 it remains intact until the end of the war, but at xv 361 ff. it is destroyed by Apollo as a sandcastle is by a child; (*c*) in xiv and xv it is sometimes present and sometimes absent. The answer to these worries is to be found in the Homeric way of telling a story. Each point is made emphatically in its own place because it is relevant to the context, and though we may complain that insufficient notice is taken of what is said elsewhere, there is no real contradiction. (*a*) vii 435 refers to no more than the strengthening of a wall which already exists; a rampart is reinforced by the addition of towers and battlements. (*b*) At xv 361 Apollo does not destroy the whole wall, but only that part where he himself is fighting, and its destruction receives full attention. (*c*) The alleged presence of the wall at some places and it absence from others are due simply to the technique of mentioning only what is immediately relevant to the action. At xii 62 Polydamas summons Hector to cross it and therefore it is mentioned, as this is a vital decision in the Trojan attack; later it is not mentioned because in the general excitement of the battle it is no longer of first interest.

The need for emphasis and simplicity may cause difficulty when an action is not really simple. This is the case with the exploits and death of Patroclus. Here there are two successive themes: first, Patroclus puts on the armour of Achilles and causes panic among the Trojans who think that Achilles has come back to battle (xvi 281–2); and second, he is himself a brilliant fighter who deserves attention for his exploits. In the end he is killed, but well before that the Trojans know who he is. In the first stage Patroclus thinks that the trick with the armour will work (xvi 40–3) and for a time it does. In the second stage the Trojans realize the truth, and Sarpedon, feeling there is something false about the man whom they believe to be Achilles, calls his bluff:

'I will go against this man, that I may find who it is that holds the field. Truly he has done much harm to the Trojans, since he has loosened the knees of many noble men.' (xvi 423–5)

At this point the deception ceases to work, and we hear no more of it. Patroclus pursues his course in his own right, but Glaucus knows who he is and urges the Trojans against him (xvi 543 ff.). The action has entered a new phase and ends with the death of Patroclus. The trick with the armour succeeded at first and then ended in disaster; each phase has its own dramatic character.

A different kind of trouble comes from the conflicting claims of traditional stories. In the course of years a story can develop in diverse ways, and we may assume that enterprising poets took pride in giving a new shape to something familiar. This would be true equally of heroic lays, such as form the stuff of the *Iliad*, and

8. *Two horse skeletons from a seventh-century tomb at Salamis. Although it was an obsolete practice in his day, Homer knew of the traditional sacrifice of horses and men in Mycenaean Greece, and may also have heard of its continued existence at Salamis in Cyprus* (see p. 49)

9, 10, 11. *Many variations of the tale of the blinding of Polyphemus were depicted across the ancient world. In the version* ABOVE *from Ionia, c. 550 B.C., and* LEFT *from Eleusis, c. 650 B.C., the instrument drawn may be a spit. In the Etruscan version* BELOW *it is clearly a stake. Homer suggested both*

of the dateless folk-tales, which do so much for the *Odyssey*. No doubt various versions of episodes were known to Homer who took his pick and shaped it to his own aim, but in one important case we can almost see how he operates at more than one layer and produces a noble result, even if not all its pieces fit exactly. In Book ix the Achaeans send an embassy to Achilles and offer him princely amends for Agamemnon's action with Briseis. The episode is essential to the whole scheme of the *Iliad*, for it hardens the quarrel and calls for still greater efforts in battle. But the original embassy may have been quite small and simple, consisting, as in the *Iliad*, of Odysseus and Aias. These remain the actual ambassadors, and are spoken of in the dual, 'The two of them went . . .' (ix 182). This is natural enough, since it is they who carry out the first duty, but to them is added a third character, who goes with them and plays a large part in the action. Phoenix is an old man who has helped to bring up Achilles and is entirely trusted by him. He tells a long and highly relevant story about Meleager and the evil effects of anger in time of war. The story adds to the richness of the poem and illustrates the heroic conception of anger when a man's pride is injured. It has even been thought that Homer got some of his wrath of Achilles from the wrath of Meleager and here pays an indirect tribute to his indebtedness. No doubt such wrath was not an uncommon theme, and different examples illustrated it. The two ambassadors are for a time overshadowed by Phoenix, but the whole plan is noble and human.

Among the age-old tales of the *Odyssey* is that of the one-eyed giant whose eye is put out by the hero whom he intends to eat. Sometimes the instrument used is the spit on which he intends to cook the hero before eating him. This is not the version in the *Odyssey*, where no spit is needed, since the hero's comrades are eaten raw, and Homer may have decided that this was even more disgusting than cooking them first. But he seems to have known the alternative version, and at one place he lets it slip in. Odysseus heats an enormous stake to put into the giant's eye, and all is straightforward until, when the stake has been heated, we hear:

But when the stake of olive-wood, was, though green, going soon to catch fire, and glowed terribly throughout . . . (9.378–9)

A stake of unseasoned wood would catch fire if left long enough in the flames, and so far the poet is impeccable, but when the stake of Odysseus gets red-hot and shines throughout, the poet has in mind not a wooden stake but an iron spit, and an alternative version has slipped into his mind. It is a small point and does not interfere with the story, but it suggests that Homer knew so many formulae that sometimes he chose one that did not exactly fit his immediate theme.

More usually Homer appreciates the differences between one version and another and makes his own use of them. Of this two notable examples must suffice. It is more than likely that in earlier songs Achilles, after killing Hector, mutilated his body. This would be known to Homer's audiences, who might expect it from him, and he takes advantage of it. When Achilles prepares to go out and fight Hector, he tells the dead Patroclus that he will bring back Hector's armour and head (xviii 334–5), and this means at least that he will behead him. When he drags the dead body behind his chariot, he plans 'shameless doings' against him (xxii 395), and a little later he declares his purpose to throw the body to the dogs (xxiii 20–1). We naturally expect that he will keep his word and there is in fact nothing very shameless about it. For on his side Hector has intended to throw the body of Patroclus to the dogs (xvii 127) and later to cut off his head and stick it on the battlements (xviii 177). We should not be surprised if the *Iliad* ended with a revengeful mutilation of Hector's body, and no doubt early versions of the story did. But Homer follows a different, more subtle plan. After suggesting a fearful vengeance, he makes Achilles yield to Priam's entreaties, and in so doing he passes beyond the legitimate heroic vengeance to something much nobler and grander. His conclusion is a surprise, magnificently calculated and achieved by using the conventional story to give a false clue.

Something of the same technique may be seen in the more

complex tales of the *Odyssey*, though here the changes are imposed by circumstance. In the world-wide tales of the Wanderer's Return is one that he was saved from the sea by the king's daughter, whom he afterwards married. The theme could not lightly be abandoned, but Odysseus, who has Penelope waiting for him at home, cannot marry a princess on the way. But Homer does not quite shirk the theme of a marriage with the young girl Nausicaa. Her approaching marriage is more than once forecast—by Athene when she appears in a dream (6.33 ff.) and by Nausicaa herself when she asks her mother for a waggon and mules for the laundry (6.66–7). When Odysseus makes his 'sweet and cunning' speech to her, he ends by hoping that the gods will grant her a happy marriage (6.180–5). When her maidens have washed and anointed him, Nausicaa says to them with charming candour:

'Would that such a man could be called my husband, dwelling here, and that it would please him to stay in this place.' (6.244–5)

and her instructions to him on how to find her home have the conscious propriety of a young woman falling in love. But it cannot go on. There is more for Odysseus to do in Phaeacia than dally with Nausicaa, and though his prowess in the sports may belong to the Wanderer's wooing of the king's daughter, Nausicaa fades from the scene. We have been led to expect that something will happen between her and Odysseus, not indeed marriage because Penelope stands in the way, but still something, and it comes in the short and touching scene, when Odysseus meets her on his way from the bath, and she says to him:

'Greeting, stranger, once you are in your own native land, may you remember me, for to me first you owe the price of your life.' (8.461–2)

Odysseus thanks her for what she has done for him, and we hear no more of her. The technique of the 'false clue' is used differently from Achilles' treatment of Hector, but no less successfully. Despite her early hopes Nausicaa is left with only the consolation that after all she saved Odysseus and that he will remember it.

Of special interest is the effect which formulae have on our response to Homeric poetry. This is particularly true of repeated lines and repeated passages, which may seem to us more apt in one place than in another and have in fact been used to argue differences between good and bad poets. A simple case is in some similes. We may not care very much if those similes which compare warriors to lions or boars or wolves occur more than once; for after all the scenes of the battlefield are themselves often repeated. But it may be matter for complaint when a simile which seems delightfully apt and lively at one place is used differently at another. For instance, at vi 506–11 Paris, running off to the battlefield, is compared with a barley-fed horse which breaks its tether and races for the pasturage of the mares. It fits at all points, and has the additional advantage that the stallion seeking the mares resembles the amorous Paris. At xv 262–8 the same simile is used of Hector, and with the first one fresh in our minds, we are surprised and a little disappointed, since it seems to be less apt for Hector than for Paris. Yet this is a wrong approach. Each simile must be taken in its own context without reference to any appearances it may have elsewhere. It derives its life and its character from its context, and we are right to associate it as closely as we can. In hearing these words about Hector we have no right to think of him as a woman-izer like Paris.

This adaptability of repeated lines can be seen nicely in a small point. After a day's heavy fighting the Trojans camp on the plain outside Troy (viii 555–8) and their camp-fires are compared with the stars about the moon on a windless night. The simile conveys a beautiful calm after the fighting and marks an interval before the next stage of action when Agamemnon sends an embassy to Achilles. Yet we may guess that it is in part formulaic, for the stars are not at their brightest when the moon is full, and in the terms of the comparison there is nothing to identify with the moon if the camp-fires are identified with the stars. The words take colour from the setting and what matters is the sense of peace. Later at xvi 297–300 there is another simile, which illustrates a scene not of calm but of carnage; as the Greek ships keep off the fire-attack on them, they are likened to Zeus gathering a great cloud on a mountain, and then two lines recur:

All the lookout-places are revealed, and the high peaks, and the valleys; and from the sky the unlimited air opens out.

Taken by itself this is entirely apt. The clearness after a thunderstorm deserves the beautiful lines and gains from them. But their main purpose is quite different from that of their earlier appearance. Here there is no case of quiet after violence, but of a special phenomenon in time of storm, of something bright and glittering and vast, but not restful or peaceful. The lines existed for use, and could be treated quite differently, but on each occasion with flawless effect.

The chamaeleonic quality of conventional sets of words appears in more unassuming ways than these. Take the phrase 'a little, not for long', which make the second half of a hexameter. It is applied first by Thetis to the brevity of Achilles' life (i 416) and in it is all the weight of his predestined doom, which haunts him and his mother. Then they are applied to Adamas, who is wounded below his navel with a spear. He gasps like an ox, and the words are applied to his last pants (xiii 573). They belong to the agonies of death, in this case merciful because they do not last long, and this is the note conveyed. Thirdly, they appear (22.473) when Odysseus hangs the faithless serving women, with nooses round their necks. They struggle with their feet, but not for long. The words come with sudden force and make the death at once horrible and pathetic, which is surely what the poet intends. An adaptable phrase of this kind can even add something to the action. We may take the line 'So spoke he, and the old man was afraid and obeyed his word.' In itself it carries a weight of meaning, but this gets a special character when it is set to work. It is applied first to the priest Chryses, when Agamemnon dismisses his entreaties for the restoration of his daughter and sends him away with a veiled threat (i 33). Chryses is so overwhelmed that words fail him but goes off to pray to Apollo for help. Much later the same words are applied to Priam after Achilles, who has treated him kindly, warns him not to provoke him (xxiv 560), and there it has an almost tragic pathos as it emphasizes the helplessness of the old man before the terrible hero, and adds yet another touch to this wonderful scene.

These two phrases contain in themselves a small element of drama which is enhanced when they are put into action. Another phrase is in itself even more colourless—'and he knew it in his heart'. When heralds come from Agamemnon to take Briseis from Achilles, he knows their purpose and feels no need to ask it (i 333); this the phrase asserts, and in doing so catches the restraint and courtesy with which Achilles greets his friends. When Zeus on Olympus finds Hera and Athene sitting apart, he knows that they are up to mischief and guesses what it is (viii 446). He is angry with them, and his anger influences what he says, but the transition is effected by this formula with perfect ease. Thirdly, when Glaucus is wounded and begs Apollo to heal his wound, the god answers his prayer. Glaucus knows it, and the words reflect his joy and gratitude (xvi 530). Lastly, when Hector knows that Athene has betrayed him and that he must fight Achilles alone (xxii 296), the formula conveys his sudden recognition of his fatal plight and strengthens his decision to fight. In these cases a single short phrase serves quite different ends according to its context, and in this there is nothing forced or artificial. The phrase takes it colour from the situation, and, being itself perfectly clear and straightforward, does not in any way conflict with the specific emotional atmosphere of each occasion.

The contextual adaptability of formulae can go further than this and achieve remarkable results on a rather larger scale. A notable case is a line which Scipio Africanus is said to have recited with deep emotion on the site of Carthage, thinking that in due course Rome would meet a like fate:

There shall be a day when holy Ilium shall perish.

Scipio gives to it his own context, and it is deeply impressive. In the *Iliad*, it is the middle of three lines:

'For well I know this in my heart, and mind; there shall be a day when

holy Ilium shall perish, and Priam, and the people of Priam of the good
ashen spear.'

This is a well-wrought passage, and it appears first at iv 163–5,
when Agamemnon, after the Trojans have broken their oath,
proclaims with confidence that none the less Troy will be destroyed. The words reflect his certainty, his assurance that Zeus will
not desert him. We feel this spirit in the words, and are right to
feel it; for they reflect what Agamemnon has in mind. Then at
vi 447–9 Hector uses the same words to Andromache, and they are
full of the pathos of his speech to her; for they reflect his certainty
that Troy will fall and that she and he and their child are doomed.
Here it has a noble, unquestioning pathos and fits perfectly into
the speech of which it is part. The names which convey to Agamemnon victims of his triumph convey to Hector the fellow
victims of his own doom. The very fact that the words are formulaic gives them an independence and integrity. We supply
some of the meaning and this is as it ought to be.

The repeated phrase is an integral part of oral poetry, and we
are wrong to say that a phrase is right in this place and wrong in
that, or that if such a phrase is repeated one case must be original
and the rest repetitious. We are equally wrong to assume that the
alleged later phrase is necessarily worse than the earlier. These
distinctions of early and late are irrelevant, and what counts is the
meaning of a phrase in its context on each appearance. Even when
a phrase marks a high point in the action, it may be repeated
elsewhere and be equally effective. For instance, when Agamemnon starts his attack on the Trojans, we hear:

Then did each man give orders to his charioteer to hold back his horses
in good order there at the ditch. (xi 47–8)

At this important moment just before the attack all must be regular
and disciplined. In the next book, when Hector is attacking the
Achaean camp, precisely the same words are used of the Trojans
(xii 84–5). But neither passage echoes the other, and each is in its
place dramatic and fully motivated.

The oral style presents other problems when we turn from its manner to its contents. Since it was formed over a long period of years, habits and usages and material objects from different centuries are crystallized in formulae. It seems that once a formula was found for a need, it continued to be used even though the habit or thing had passed away. It may not have been understood very clearly, but it was sufficiently intelligible to meet a need in the narrative. Then as time passed and bards introduced new formulae for new customs, these found a place at the side of the older, outdated customs, which were preserved in words and must have still conveyed some sort of meaning.

The obvious place for such a mixture is in accounts of battle and what belongs to it. Arms and armour are indispensable to the story and must always be intelligible, though occasionally they may be unusual and call for special attention. In dealing with them the Homeric tradition seems to reflect three successive periods, and to preserve something from each. In the far distance is the armour of the fourteenth century, of which scattered relics survived in formulae fashioned at the time. This was when a man's chief defence was a large shield, which protected his whole body and behind which he operated by throwing a spear, wearing no armour on his body. Minoan in origin, this was also Mycenaean. Homer shows indisputable traces of it in the shield of Aias 'like a tower' (vii 219; xi 485; xvii 128), which he uses consistently. No doubt this belonged to Aias from the start and continued to be his when habits had changed. But slighter traces of it in others can be seen when a warrior is said to advance 'moving step by step under his shield' (xiii 158, 807; xvi 609), or the shield has the epithet 'reaching to his feet' (xv 646), or a warrior trips over it as he runs (xv 645–6). These formulae are useful to the narrative and their sense is not examined too closely. They are perfectly intelligible and suit their contexts. Mycenaean art sometimes depicts a helmet made of boars' teeth, and such teeth have not uncommonly been found in graves. This helmet, common at one time, seems to have gone out of use about 1300, but memories of it remained in words, and there is a precise description of such a helmet when Odysseus

12. *A fourteenth-century Minoan helmet made of bronze, the knob pierced for the crest*

13, 14. RIGHT: *a boar's tusk helmet, reconstructed from remains at Knossos.* BELOW: *a Mycenaean warrior carrying a large shield and wearing a boar's tusk helmet (see pp. 46–7, 146)*

15, 16. *By the time of the Trojan War, shields became smaller as body armour came into use, and were often made of leather* (RIGHT, ABOVE: *the Warrior Vase,* C. 1200 B.C.). *Homer, however, prefers to dress his warriors in the traditional bronze. On the Rhodian plate* RIGHT, C. 700 B.C., *Hector and Menelaus wear metal corslets behind their small shields*

goes out on night-operations (x 261–5). In the setting it is an heirloom and a rarity, and it is just conceivable that the poet may have seen an actual example. It is more likely that the tradition preserved a formulaic account of it, and that it was regarded as something rather special to be reserved for unusual occasions. This is the oldest piece of armour in the poems, and it appears only once.

A second stage began historically about 1300 when the Mycenaean Greeks reformed their system of armour by distributing the weight more evenly with an eye to greater mobility. The big shield disappeared, and its functions were taken over by a smaller, round shield, some kind of body-armour and greaves. On the whole this is what Homer's predecessors established as the armour of the heroic age, and as such Homer depicts it regularly. The shield is commonly 'round' or 'well-balanced'; warriors wear a cuirass which is sometimes made of metal and never explicitly of anything else, except for Aias, son of Oïleus (ii 529) and some allies of the Trojans (ii 830), whose cuirasses are of linen. The Achaeans are called 'well-greaved' and less commonly 'bronze-greaved', and this was true of them in the thirteenth century but not again till the seventh. Homer is unsure how greaves were used and makes little play with them. Tradition insisted that he should make all weapons of bronze, and this he unfailingly does, both in single weapons and in general epithets such as 'bronze-corsleted' (iv 448; viii 62), or 'bronze-helmeted' (v 699; vi 398 etc.), or 'bronze-plated' of helmets (xii 183; xvii 294; xx 397). Homer knows about iron and the trade in it (1.184), but he confines it to tools and never uses it for weapons. But he knows, from his own world, that it is a material for destruction, for he has a formulaic phrase 'for of itself iron draws on a man' (16.294; 19.13), which means that the mere sight of weapons excites men to use them. Homer goes against his own time in his consistent use of bronze and suggests that this is indispensable to any conception of the heroic age.

The Homeric treatment of the dead must owe a lot to the poetical tradition. They were normally cremated, as Anticlea,

17. *The moulded corslet and helmet of a Greek foot soldier or hoplite. Dated at approximately 700 B.C., this is the earliest known example of hoplite armour.*

mother of Odysseus, says that she was (11.220), and there is a full-scale cremation of Patroclus in Book xxiii. Yet there are hints of a different practice. First, a word is used in general by Hector (vii 85) and specifically of Sarpedon (xvi 456, 674), which seems to mean 'embalm'. This would accord with a Mycenaean practice, since remains of an embalmed body were found by Schliemann in Shaft Grave V at Mycenae. It seems too that honey was used in the process, and this may be why, when Patroclus is burned, two great jars of honey and unguents are set against his pyre (xxiii 170), and Achilles himself was burned with 'plenty of unguents and sweet honey' (24.67). These are the merest hints, and suggest that Homer did not really know about embalming. Tradition preserved echoes of it, but they meant little to him. What he understood was cremation.

This is unexpected because cremation seems to have been rare except between about 1200 and 800. It hardly existed before this, and afterwards it passed out of use. Homer's use of it indicates that the tradition which he inherited gained strength in this period. It may indeed be the case that Attica, which was the mother of the Ionian people before it emigrated to Asia Minor, was a powerful force in the growth of heroic song and the first source of certain formulae. It was at least a place where cremation was practised in these dark ages, and that may have stimulated the creation of formulaic phrases for cremation thereafter applicable to any funeral. Intrusions from his own age, when burial was usual, are few and faint, but worth a mention. Menelaus delays on his way home from Troy for the death of his helmsman, 'that he might bury a comrade' (3.285). But though bodies were buried under mounds, there was no reason why ashes also should not be, and so in fact they were for Hector (xxiv 797 ff.), Elpenor (12.11 ff.) and Achilles (24.76 ff.).

Homer reflects that stage in the tradition when stock themes of heroic song, like funerals, had been systematized to suit a certain phase of culture, and once the words had been found for them these could be used again. Nor would the idea of cremation have caused any difficulty to those who had never witnessed it but could easily imagine it. Tradition certainly preserved elements from an early age which enriched accounts of funerals, and themselves reflected the actual practice of the Mycenaean age. At the pyre of Patroclus, Achilles sacrifices four horses, nine dogs, and twelve young men (xxiii 171 ff.). This is a tremendous occasion, and Homer not only treats it fully but in the case of the young men gives notice in advance (xviii 336; xxi 27 ff.), as if it were something very special and characteristic of Achilles' fury. In fact this is Homer's way of explaining a difficult element in the tradition. Human beings were in fact sacrificed, as we know from graves at Dendra, Asine, and Mycenae, before 1200. From fact they passed into tradition and Homer humanely explains them as best he can. Dogs were buried with their masters at almost all dates and call for no special notice; horses were sacrificed on the mainland throughout the Mycenaean age. The tradition was strong and based on fact; Homer or some predecessor alters it only by substituting cremation for burial. He may even have heard of exceptional practices on the periphery of the Greek world in his own day. In Cyprus, at Salamis and Enkomi, sacrifices, including men and horses, are made as late as the middle of the seventh century. Cyprus, which was colonized by Achaeans about 1200, kept some of their customs for a long time. It is not impossible that Homer knew of this and was reassured by it in dealing with heroic funerals.

Distinctive levels of time can be seen in other, less important matters, and then we may assume that Homer follows tradition without worrying too much what it means and certainly without making special concessions to it. This is the case with the two different ways of taking women in marriage, the one by paying for a wife with a bride-price, the other by demanding a dowry with her. To the first class belong Hector, who took his wife from the halls of Eëtion, 'when he had paid countless bride-gifts' (xxii 472), Iphidamas, who is killed before he brought his wife home, 'though he gave a great price for her' (xi 243), and Othryoneus, who wished to marry Cassandra and gave free service in war instead of paying money (xiii 366). This is the method of the gods.

When Aphrodite is false to Hephaestus, he vows that he will keep her in prison until her father returns all the bride-gifts (8.319). On the other hand Homer knows also of a quite different system. Laothoe, who marries Priam, comes with a rich dowry from her father (xxii 51), and when Agamemnon offers Achilles one of his daughters, he promises a dowry with her (ix 146 ff.). Bride-price and dowry are quite different. The first may be the older and come from a time when women were rare because many of them were exposed after birth. Their value was calculated in cattle, and they received such names as Alphesiboia, 'winner of cattle', Phereboia, 'bringer of cattle'; and Polyboia, 'worth many cattle'. A fine woman commanded a high price, and Aristotle remarks that in primitive Greece men 'bought their women from one another' (*Politics* 1268ᵇ 40). When women were less frequently exposed after birth, their parents could get rid of them by paying a price to intending husbands.

The two systems may conceivably have overlapped in a single society, and the prevalence of one or the other have come from local conditions. But on the whole it looks as if bride-price were more primitive than dowry. It is practised by the gods, and knowledge of it may have survived because of the importance of some marriages in a heroic society. The theme is not one of great importance, and it is natural that the tradition is not consistent on it and allows two competing sets of formulae. Nor is Homer himself very clear about it. When Athene lays down a policy for the Suitors of Penelope, she suggests that there must be gifts in plenty 'such as are fit to go with a dear daughter' (1.278), and when Eurymachus tells Telemachus what to do with his mother, he makes the same suggestion in very much the same words (2.197). The context leaves no doubt that Penelope is to bring a dowry with her, and in this we may see the conditions of Homer's own time. But the word that he uses in both passages is *eëdna*, which means 'bride-price'. There is certainly some confusion, and it is possible that in fashioning words for a dowry that would suit the traditional language, some bard, even Homer himself, used the old word for bride-price in the new sense of dowry. The word was not very common, and it was easy to think that it referred simply to financial transactions in connection with marriage.

These three cases, armour, cremation and matrimonial finance, show in descending order of importance how a changing custom can both be adapted to poetry and still keep some of its first character. The more important it is, the more strict attention Homer pays to it.

The different layers of habits and objects in the Homeric poems reflect the long process of their growth. In general we may distinguish three periods, each of which makes its own contribution. The first and oldest derives from the Mycenaean civilization and reaches its historical conclusion about 1200. To this period belongs the Trojan War, and in it posterity set the heroic age. From it survive certain memories frozen into formulaic words and though, outside battle, these are not very numerous they are distinctive and authentic. On the whole they seem to have survived for their intrinsic interest, for the light they throw on this or that aspect of the heroic age. Such are sword-hilts riveted with silver (ii 45; iii 334; xvi 135), silver work inlaid with gold and enamel as on the shield of Achilles, palaces with upper floors and with rooms opening on vestibules and courtyards, open precincts for gods instead of roofed temples, Nestor's cup with its images of doves (xi 632 ff.), Penelope's throne made of ivory and silver (19.55). More remarkable is the knowledge of Egyptian Thebes (ix 381–3) as it was in the fourteenth century, before strangers were excluded from Egypt, and almost to this date belongs Nestor's exceptional advice that chariots should be used not merely for transport but to charge in line, as happened at the battle of Kadesh in 1288 between the Hittites and the Egyptians. These are mere flotsam and jetsam from the remote past, but they reinforce the consistent account of late Mycenaean arms and armour and the general impression of strong and wealthy kingdoms.

The second period comes from what may be called the Dark Age of Greece between *c.* 1200 and *c.* 800. It was when the Mycenaean system broke up and from a general turmoil a new

Greece was slowly born, when colonists from the mainland took its traditions oversea to Ionia, when the old official script was lost and writing was unknown. Heroic song, which had been born in the Mycenaean age, must at this time have developed its full character as a record of a glorious past and canonized men and events of that time. The epic style must have been vastly enriched and enlarged and adapted, shaping new formulae and preparing itself for new themes. Inevitably it admits new elements from its own time, but they are not of first importance, and clearly the bards honoured the past more than the present. To it belong the use of chariots as means of transport from one part of the battle-field to another, the carrying by warriors of two light spears such as are depicted on Geometric vases, the mixture of peoples, including Dorians, in Crete (19.172–6), the notion that Egypt is so far away that it takes even birds a year to cross the sea to it (3.320–2), the part played by the Phoenicians as ubiquitous traders and slavers. This is not much, but such as it is, it illustrates how Greek heroic song throve by taking note of its own times to supplement the past and give a greater reality to it.

The third period is roughly that of the century or so in which the Homeric poems were composed. If they come from the latter part of it, we may date it as from 800 to 700 or later. It was a period of great changes, and amongst much else it saw the introduction of the new Greek alphabet. Of this the poems say nothing, and their only reference to writing treats it as something remote and mysterious, as indeed the Mycenaean script would seem to the Dark Age (vi 168–9). This age introduces into the poems some features of its own—the wealth of Apollo's shrine at Delphi (ix 404–5), the seated image of Athene (vi 303), the wheeled tripods of Hephaestus (xviii 373 ff.), the first appearance of the hoplite phalanx in battle (xiii 130 ff.; xvi 214 ff.), the Gorgon on the shield of Agamemnon (xi 36), possibly the brooch of Odysseus with its two sheathes or tubes (19.226 ff.). The several layers of culture in the poems come from the different ages in which the tradition was at work assimilating and creating. There are inevitable inconsistencies and contradictions between earlier and later usages, but there is little confusion. Though the long succession of poets made many changes and innovations in the repertory of material details, they kept the main appearance harmonious. They did not try to make everything conform to a single age, past or present, but presented a picture sufficiently coherent and intelligible to be a solid background for heroic actions.

CHAPTER FOUR

Devices of Composition

THE oral poet must at all costs catch and keep the attention of his audience. This means both that he omits much that a literate poet might think necessary and that he employs certain devices to make his narrative easy to follow. His task is to keep every action as clear as possible and not to encumber it with secondary considerations. To make sure that his hearers follow him he has, as it were, to take them into his confidence and to act on the assumption that they know all that he knows and do not require explanation of many small points in the story. This is a trick, for the poet has not explained these points but expects them to be picked up as he goes on, and acts as if he had already spoken of them. Something of this kind is needed to avoid questions and explanations in the middle of the narrative and charm the audience into a receptive mood. Homer's method is to make his listeners participate in his creation by supplying certain explanations which would otherwise interrupt the flow of the narrative. As the Alexandrian scholar Aristarchus said: 'The poet endows his heroic characters with the knowledge which he himself possesses' (Scholl. BT ad xvi 844).

This saves a lot of trouble. Opponents on the battlefield know each other, and though this is perfectly natural in the tenth year of war, it would be no less necessary in the first year if we are to be spared too many introductions. Sthenelus knows Pandarus (v 246); Diomedes knows Dolon (x 447); Aias and Menelaus know Archelochus and Euphorbus (xiv 472; xvii 23). When Idomeneus and Achilles exult over the deaths of Othryoneus and Iphition, they know the details of their lives, which the poet has just related (xiii 374–6; xix 389–92). This hardly calls for notice, but the same

18, 19. *Treasures from sixteenth-century Mycenae.* RIGHT: *the Lion Hunt dagger, inlaid with silver, gold and niello (see pp. 51, 87), and* FAR RIGHT *a silver and gold pin with a Cretan figure as decoration.*

20. *In one of the shaft graves of Mycenae Schliemann found a small gold goblet with handles, decorated with images of two doves. Although much smaller than the one Homer describes, and with two and not four handles, this is possibly 'Nestor's cup' of the* Iliad *(see p. 51)*

technique is used more subtly when a character speaks with knowledge of something which he has had no chance of learning.
Achilles cannot have heard that Chryses has prayed to Apollo
(i 380), nor Diomedes that Achilles will not carry out his threat to
sail home the next day (ix 701–3). Even the gods are subjected to
this treatment. Calypso tells Odysseus to build a raft, since this is
what Zeus has instructed Hermes to tell her, but Hermes has in
fact omitted this part of his message (5.33, 112).

This device sometimes pierces deep into the plot and reveals its
usefulness. In the underworld the ghosts of Odysseus' mother,
Anticlea, and of Agamemnon speak of Telemachus as a grown
man, though at the time he cannot be more than thirteen or
fourteen (11.185–7, 449). The audience, who by now know Telemachus well, think of him as a young man, and since nothing is
gained by disturbing them, he is so presented. When Eumaeus
tells Penelope that the Beggar (the disguised Odysseus) has spent
three days and three nights in his steading (17.515), he has actually
spent four, but we remember three days and nights because they
are full of action and talk, while the fourth is empty. Therefore
it is quietly omitted. The poet is constantly aware of the dangers
of saying too much and adapts his narrative to the need of holding
his audience.

Homer aims at a continuous flow of narrative, and it is notable
that when certain actions are necessary to the plot but not in
themselves very attractive, he supplies some other action contemporary with them but more interesting. He seems to have seen
that this was a chance for effects which might not otherwise fall into his hands. In Book iii there is some delay when Hector sends
heralds to Troy to arrange for the duel between Paris and Menelaus, and while this lasts, Homer presents Helen on the walls of
Troy where she identifies the Achaean leaders to Priam (121–244).
After this the heralds are ready for the sacrifices and the taking of
oaths. In Book vi Hector has to go to Troy to arrange for an
offering to Athene, and in this interval Homer gives the delightful
interchange between Glaucus and Diomedes (vi 119–236).
Immediately after it we revert to Hector's visit to Troy. In Book

xxiii Achilles, who has killed Hector, prepares to burn the body of
Patroclus, but Homer does not move straight to this. In the night
before the rites Achilles at last falls into a deep sleep, in which
Patroclus appears to him. This fills the time-gap, but it does
a great deal more (xxiii 62–102). It takes the place of a farewell between the two friends, which did not happen when Achilles
sent off Patroclus to battle and death in Book xvi. In such cases
Homer takes advantage of an opportunity for a new theme,
which is important in itself and deserves the care which he gives
to it.

The poet holds his audience by the reality and solidity of his
narrative, and to maintain this he resorts to a constant, lively
invention, especially of small touches which do not much affect
the main story. There is no need to think that they are drawn
from an amorphous mass of saga or even from other poets. Their
task is to enliven a tale so crowded with persons that they may
easily become faint or tedious. This is specially the case in the
battle-scenes where many are killed or wounded and must be
given momentary attention. This is secured by some small touch
of information. Axylus lives in Arisbe and welcomes all who pass
by on the road (vi 13–15): Meges wears a breastplate from Ephyra
(xv 530 ff.); Iphition was born in a rich land under snowy Tmolus
(xx 382 ff.); the priestess Theano has nursed the bastard Pedaeus
(v 70); Othryoneus, killed by Idomeneus, was promised the
hand of Cassandra by Priam (xiii 361–9); Menesthius, one of
Achilles' Myrmidons, is the son of a river and the grandson
of Peleus (xvi 173 ff.); Iphidamas, son of the Trojan Antenor,
has been brought up in Thrace and come to Troy with twelve
ships, where he is killed by Agamemnon (xi 221 ff,). Even in
the *Odyssey*, where there is no battlefield, such small touches
are not lacking. Aegyptius is bent with age, and his son has been
eaten by the Cyclops (2.15 ff.); Elpenor was not brave in war nor
strong in his wits (10.552–3); Euryalus was the second best-looking
man in Phaeacia (8.115–17). These touches are surely inventions,
devised to create interest in minor characters.

In the same spirit Homer introduces small details of action

which enliven the narrative. He suggests that there is more in a situation than meets the eye. There is no need to assume that these come from some other version of the story. No doubt there were many such versions, but these cases serve an immediate single purpose and are quite at home where they are placed. So before his duel with Paris, Menelaus insists on an oath because Priam's sons are not to be trusted (iii 106). Its task is to motivate what would be otherwise a stock theme, and in this context it is human and convincing. On Olympus Hera speaks of the trouble she had in collecting a host to fight against Priam (iv 25 ff.). Of course this might refer to Hera's connection with Argos and come from another cycle, but in its place it serves an adequate purpose by strengthening her appeal for help against the Trojans. Similar circumstantial inventions appear when Andromache tells Hector that the Achaeans have assaulted Troy three times at a certain place (vi 435 ff.), or Aeneas lags behind because he is angry with Priam (xiii 459 ff.), or Achilles says that his mother foretold the death of Patroclus (xviii 9), or the Phaeacian ship carrying Odysseus finds the harbour of Phorcys in Ithaca because the sailors have been there before (13.113), or Antinous says that there is no man like Odysseus because he remembers him from childhood (21.95). Such small touches strengthen the impression of a crowded world of events around the main story, and this is their purpose. There is no need to see more in them, or to treat them as anything else but artistic detail.

Since the poet composes on a large scale he sometimes marks main features in advance by forecast or prophecy. This may do no more than keep us informed of what is going to happen, as when Athene tells Achilles that he will receive threefold recompense— an understatement—for Agamemnon's treatment of him (i 213 ff.), or the poet announces that the time has come for Odysseus to return home (1.16 ff.). Forecasts may also refer to the immediate future, as when we hear that Hector will set fire to the Achaean ships (xv 596 ff.), or Penelope prays that her son may be saved, and the poet adds: 'and the goddess listened to her prayer' (4.767). Conversely, the hopes of men are sometimes shown to be futile.

When Agamemnon hopes to capture Troy on the next day and
when Achaeans and Trojans hope that the duel between Menelaus
and Paris will end the war, their disappointment is curtly stated:
'And not yet did the son of Cronus accomplish it for him (them)'
(ii 419; iii 302). Impressively central actions like the death of
Patroclus and the slaughter of the Suitors are forecast more than
once, and each forecast enhances the tragic or sinister character
of what is coming. The death of Patroclus is first mentioned when,
in answer to the summons of Achilles, he comes out of his tent,
'and it was the beginning of evil for him' (xi 604). Then Zeus tells
Hera that Patroclus will be killed by Hector (xv 65–6). Later,
when he begs Achilles to let him go to battle, the poet underlines
the significance of the event:

So, in his great foolishness, he spoke in prayer; for he was to ask for
himself an evil death and doom. (xvi 46–7)

Finally, when Achilles prays to Zeus that the Trojans may be
driven from the ships and Patroclus come home safe, we hear that
Zeus grants the first part of the prayer but not the second (xvi
248–52). So too with the Suitors. Their doom is first forecast
when Athene tells Telemachus that Odysseus will certainly
return (1.203); it is explicitly foretold at the Ithacan assembly
when the seer Halitherses interprets the action of birds (2.163 ff.);
Menelaus says that it will come to pass (4.333); Theoclymenus
sees an omen of it in an eagle holding a dove (15.525), and pro-
phesies it in dark and splendid words when the Suitors at their
wine are struck to temporary madness (20.351 ff.). Forecasts help
to keep a long story together, but also increase the tension of some
main events, which gain from being adumbrated in advance.

Aristarchus noted that Homer uses a device of 'the last thing
first' (*Ox. Pap.* 1086 on ii 763), and this was known to Cicero (*Ad
Att.* 1.16.1). In other words, when a series of questions is posed or
a list of instructions given, the answers and the performances come
in exactly the reverse order. This shows a nice understanding of
the human mind, which clings to the last thing it has heard and
works backward from it. This is by no means an exclusively

Homeric device, but abounds in the heroic poetry of other times and countries. In a Jugoslav lay the Sultan orders that no man shall drink wine in Ramadan, or wear green apparel, or gird on a sword, or dance with women; then we hear that Marko the King's son dances with women, girds on a sword, wears green apparel, and drinks in Ramadan. A much more elaborate case comes from the Assyrian version of *Gilgamesh*. Gilgamesh wishes to call up the ghost of his dead comrade Enkidu. He cunningly asks how to avoid being haunted by the dead and is given a long list of instructions, all of which he disobeys, in precisely the opposite order to that in which they are given. Homer practises this device in more than one way. When at the end of the Catalogue of the Achaean Ships he asks (*a*) who was the best fighter, and (*b*) who had the best horses, he answers in the reverse order that (*a*) the best horses were those of Eumelus (ii 763–7), and (*b*) the best warrior was Aias so long as Achilles abstained from battle (ii 768–9). This is a very simple case, but Homer, like the author of *Gilgamesh*, knew how to put the device to more elaborate service. When Odysseus speaks to the ghost of his mother, he asks her seven questions about the manner of her death, and she answers them in exactly the opposite order with the splendid climax:

'The far-sighted Shooter of Arrows did not attack me in my halls with her gentle shafts, nor did disease assail me, which most often takes away life from the limbs with hateful wasting; but longing for you and your clever ways, glorious Odysseus, and your gentleness of heart took away my honey-sweet life.' (11 197–203)

With equal ingenuity the device helps to introduce Odysseus, as yet unknown, to the Phaeacians. The queen Arete asks him, when he arrives in her palace, (*a*) who is he, (*b*) where did he get his garments, (*c*) did he not say that he came wandering over the sea. He answers the last question first, and then explains that he got his garments from the queen's daughter, but the third question is not answered till much later, and the Phaeacians must stay in ignorance while he makes his full impression on them.

Heroic poetry runs the risk of being monotonous because it is set very much in a single key and deals extensively with violent actions. These have their own keen appeal, but something is needed to throw a distinguishing light on them and to reveal unsuspected qualities. This is done by similes, which occur in nearly all such poetry. A simile is a metaphor extended and simplified. Metaphor expresses what cannot be said fully in a direct statement; simile illuminates a direct statement by drawing attention to special aspects of it. In oral heroic lays similes are usually short and pointed, as when in *Gilgamesh* the hero weeps for his dead comrade 'like a lioness robbed of her cubs', or in the Flood bodies glut the seas 'like fish-spawn', or the gods come to a sacrifice 'like flies'. In Jugoslav lays women lament 'like cuckoos' or hiss 'like a furious serpent', while warriors are 'like burning coals' or 'mountain wolf-packs'; eyes pierce through the darkness 'like a prowling wolf's at midnight' or a horse races 'like a star across the cloudless heavens'. The Kirghiz commonly compare warriors to leopards or camels or tigers or bears; words are like hawks; a woman's eyes sparkle like mirrors. For the Kalmucks a woman's face is like the full moon, dust rises like the white clouds of the sky, a hero is beautiful as the meeting of friends. Examples can be found everywhere and illustrate how a new note is for a moment given to a recited lay by an image that does not belong to its immediate ambience. Such similes are usually short, and of these there are many examples in Homer. A shield is 'like a tower', which means that it is Mycenaean, and the image comes from the far past. Thetis rises from the sea 'like a mist' (i 359); Apollo descends 'like the night' (i 47); warriors are 'like lions or boars' (v 782–3; vii 256–7). This is the simplest form. It is what we find in other countries and may be the earliest form in Greece, since it is a natural way to express a resemblance. It presupposes an identity between what are otherwise heterogeneous objects. For a moment we see something in a new light, and once such an art is established it is natural to develop and enrich it.

Homer avoids two uses of simile which are found to some degree elsewhere. The first is the so-called 'negative simile', favoured by the Slavonic peoples, in which the individuality of a person or an action is emphasized by the statement that he is *not* something else, though it might be thought that he is. The second in the rapid accumulation of short similes round a single point, as when Gilgamesh denounces the goddess Ishtar with nine brief and abusive comparisons, or a Kirghiz poet praises a woman with seven very brief items in the catalogue of her beauties. Homer does neither of these things, but instead he does what is very rarely done elsewhere; he favours a full-length simile extending to six or seven lines. In this he begins by describing a scene or an action suggested by what happens in the narrative, and he then develops a complete little picture which lives for its own sake as well as for what it illustrates.

This kind of simile has few close parallels in other oral heroic poetry, and looks like a specially Greek device which appealed greatly to Homer. Such a simile begins by describing a scene suggested by the main action. But once it gets started it tends to go its own way and lose contact with what it is meant to illustrate. For instance, when Hermes is sent by the gods to Calypso on her remote island, he takes his staff and, starting from Pieria, drops down to the sea:

He hastened over the wave like a bird, a gull, which over the strange hollows of the unharvested sea looks for fish and wets its thick feathers in the salt water. (5.51–3)

The actual point of comparison is that Hermes flies over the waves like a gull, but the picture is prolonged, and nothing that Hermes does is illuminated by the gull looking for fish or wetting its feathers. Again, when Menelaus is wounded in the thigh, the visible effect of his wound is carefully delineated:

As when a Maeonian or Carian woman stains ivory with purple, to be a cheek-piece for horses; it lies in a chamber, and many horsemen desire to use it, but it lies there as a delight to the king, to be both an ornament to the horses and a glory to the driver. (iv 141–5)

The comparison is purely of visual effect, of what a fresh wound looks like, and up to this point it is apt and striking. But the rest has no bearing on the wound, which awakes neither envy nor delight. Homer often lets a simile continue on its own way after fulfilling its first need, and by this means he introduces a fresh element into his story. Our minds are turned for a moment from the blood and violence of battle to another order of things. This is so common in Homer that we surmise that he needed the similes if only because he could put into them a kind of poetry which did not fall easily into his main narrative, and that this was why he developed them on this scale.

Homer's similes are never drawn from the legendary past as his main stories are, and they are hardly drawn even from myth or theology. The only example of the first is when Penelope's lamentations are compared with those of the 'daughter of Pandareos', who is the nightingale, for her son, Itylus (19.518–23). The nearest approach to theology is when a hero is compared to Ares or 'the Lord of the war-cry' (xii 130; xx 46; ii 651; vii 166; viii 264; xviii 259). Agamemnon resembles Poseidon in his chest and Zeus in his eyes and head (ii 478–9). But except for these rare and brief cases the gods are avoided, and Homer's similes come from the world which he knew. They cover most aspects of it, from the stars in the sky to the fish in the sea, from men and women of every age and class to animals wild and domesticated, trees and flowers, the sea in all its moods and those who sail on it. No doubt this wide range had its roots in tradition, but it surely reflects Homer's own passionate interest in his world and his desire to use it as a counterweight to his heroic tale. His similes do not add to his central themes; they illustrate them and set them in new perspectives which are delightfully unexpected and engaging for their own sake.

Homer draws his similes alike from nature, animate or inanimate, and from human beings. He sees nature as it is, without attributing human qualities in some 'pathetic fallacy' and without discerning gods at work in it except in a very general way, as when Zeus thunders or Poseidon stirs the sea. In dealing with human beings he hardly ever refers to the princes and nobles who were presumably his patrons, and when once he does refer to them, it is to say that the giving of unjust judgments causes storms to come from Zeus in autumn (xvi 384–92). His skill at varying his battle-scenes by turning the attention to something quite distant does not mean that his similes are not splendidly apt. He suggests the violence of a warrior's onslaught by comparing it with the onset of natural forces, as when the Achaeans advancing to war are like a wave stirred by the west wind (iv 422–6), or the armies meeting are like two mountain-streams joining (iv 452–5), or Diomedes in action is like the flaming star of autumn (v 5–6) or a river in spate (v 87–92), or Agamemnon is like a lion that breaks in his teeth the young of a deer (xi 113–19), or the Trojans are like hounds in pursuit of a wild boar (xi 414–18) or jackals in pursuit of a wounded hind (xi 474–81). Conversely, when attack meets a resolute defence, it is like waves breaking in vain on a rocky reef (xv 618–21), or Aias stands on the defensive as a lion protects its young (xvii 133–6). Similes from winds and waves, from lions and wolves and wild boars are Homer's favourite method for conveying the primaeval, savage, instinctive violence of attack.

In these cases, and there are many of them, the Homeric simile emphasizes the force and fury of warriors, and this is no doubt ancient, since in the cut of their beards the princes of Mycenae tended to stress their likeness or kinship to lions. But Homer has moved beyond this straightforward art and often achieves subtle and unforseen effects. When Aias retreats slowly and unwillingly and obstinately, he is compared with an ass which has strayed into a barleyfield and is driven out by boys with difficulty and much breaking of sticks (xi 558–62). When Achilles appears on the rampart, a divine light shines on his head and his mere appearance gives hope to the Achaeans, and this is compared with the fires that shine from a beleaguered city and signal its need for help (xviii 207–13). When Gorgythion is killed, his head droops on one side 'like a poppy in a garden, weighed down with fruit and spring rains' (viii 305–6), and a new pathos is given to death. The macabre paradoxes of war are illumined when Patroclus derides the smitten Cebriones by comparing him to a man diving for oysters (xvi 745 ff.), or when the dying Harpalion lies 'stretched out like a worm on the earth' (xiii 655–6). There is a similar grue-some precision when the serving-women strung up by Odysseus are like thrushes or doves (22.468–9). Nor are these surprises lacking on more gentle occasions. When the old men of Troy gossip on the city-wall they sound like cicadas on a tree in a wood (iii 151–3); Iris falls into the sea like a leaden fishing-hook on a fitting of horn (xxiv 80–2).

Similes have a special use for some of the more fearsome or more gruesome episodes by bringing them closer to common experience. When Priam enters the tent of Achilles to ransom his son's body, without a word he grasps his knees and kisses his hand

as when heavy doom has fallen on a man who has killed someone in his own land, and he comes to the domain of others, even of a rich man, and amazement holds them as they look on him. (xxiv 480–2)

The comparison is surprising because Priam is compared to a murderer on the run, but it is entirely relevant, for Priam's arrival is as unexpected as that of a murderer, and the atmosphere is of bloodshed and death. Again, when Odysseus and his companions put out the single eye of the Cyclops, this has to be made actual. So, as the stake is inserted, the eye sizzles

as when a smith dips a great axe or an adze in cold water, and tempers it, it cries out loudly. (9.391–2)

This touch brings the action home. Later, when Odysseus strings the great bow, at which everyone else has failed, he does so with consummate ease:

As when a man who is well skilled in the harp and song stretches easily a string about a new peg after lopping the twisted sheep-gut at both ends. (21.406–8)

This makes the action seem perfectly normal, and sets it easily in the sequence of events. It gives too a hint that the man who can string a bow is like a musician, and this is picked up when Odysseus tests the string with his right hand and it gives a note like a swallow's (21.411). The simile catches the temper of the occasion and illuminates it.

The similes play a part in the structure of the narrative. Though the *Iliad* has four times as many as the *Odyssey*, that is because it is so much occupied with battle-scenes, where they are needed to break the monotony, and there are in consequence 164 in battle-scenes and 38 outside them. They mark specially pauses or changes in the action. When Diomedes starts his exploits, his head is like the bright star of autumn (v 5); when Hector and Paris go to join the Trojans, they come like a breeze to tired mariners (vii 4–6); the embassy to Achilles begins by comparing the divided minds of the Achaeans with a sea driven by contrary winds (ix 4–7); the fatal adventure of Patroclus starts with his tears falling like a stream from a rock (xvi 3–4); the last fight between Achilles and Hector is heralded by the Trojans flying like frightened fawns (xxii 1); the release of Odysseus from Ogygia is started by Hermes flying like a sea-bird (5.51–3); Odysseus' first sight of Phaeacia cheers him as the sons of a sick father are cheered when he begins to recover (5.394–7); the beginning of Eumaeus' exploits with Telemachus is like the meeting of a father with a son who has been long away (16.17–19); when Odysseus approaches his final action against the Suitors, he turns his thoughts this way and that, like a man turning a blood-sausage over a fire (20.25–7); when the climax at last comes, he strings the great bow as a harper strings his harp (21.406–9).

A similar desire to mark a pause or to make an emphasis may be seen in those passages where Homer accumulates similes. At ii 455 ff. the advancing Achaeans are compared successively to fire, birds and flies, and immediately afterwards their leaders sort them out as a herdsman sorts his goats, and Agamemnon is like the bull in the herd. Each of the three first similes has a different import. The fire gives the glitter of the Achaeans' arms and armour, the birds their noise and number, the flies the crowded impetus of their advance. The next two serve a different purpose by marking the occasion as one of great brilliance and importance, for it is the marshalling of the Achaean host. Hitherto we have had only single personalities, now we have a whole army. So at other crises of the poem Homer marks them by similar accumulations. At iv 422 ff., where the two hostile armies first meet, there are three similes in thirty lines; the first presents the advancing Achaeans as waves breaking on a promontory, the second the Trojans as ewes in a rich man's stable, the third the meeting of the two armies as the meeting of two mountain torrents in a dell. Again at xvii 722 ff., where the fighting reaches its climax before the intervention of Achilles, there are no less than five similes for the fighting over the body of Patroclus. Homer accumulates similes to mark important changes of direction in the main action, and though he does not do this in the *Odyssey* that is because, with its lack of battle-scenes, it does not need so to differentiate the stages of its action.

Though Homer does not pile up short similes in rapid succession, as some oral poets do in other countries, he sometimes illuminates a single scene with more than one simile, and this has the effect of presenting it from different aspects. When Sarpedon is killed by Patroclus, he is first like a tall tree cut down to be a ship's timber (xvi 482–4), then like a great bull slaughtered among his cows by a lion (xvi 487–9). The first gives his youthful grace and elegance, the second his formidable strength as he dies fighting for his people. When Hector leads an attack on the Achaeans, he is compared first to a huntsman urging on his dogs (xi 292–3), then to a storm falling on the sea (xi 297–8). The first gives his power of command in attack, the second the sudden, overwhelming strength of his onslaught. Polypoetes and Leonteus the guardians of the Achaean camp, are compared first to tall, deep-rooted oaks withstanding the wind and the rain (xii 132–4), then, as danger comes closer, and they rush to meet it, to wild boars surprised by hunters in their lair (xii 147–50). The change of action requires a change of similes. When the eye of the Cyclops is put out with a burning stake, the act is compared to a man boring a ship's timber with a drill (9.383–6), and this gives the merciless mechanism of the action, but then the sound of it is like that of a smith plunging an axe or an adze into cold water to temper it and give it strength (9.391–3).

The devices which we have examined were meant to help oral performance, and would be equally useful in short and in long poems. But when a bard changed from short poems to long, he had to assimilate his technique to rather different conditions. Since Homer's imaginary bards indicate that short lays were normal, we expect the short lay to leave traces of itself in longer poems, and this it does. Certain episodes have the completeness and independence of single lays, and suggest that Homer was well at home in this art when he worked on a larger scale. We can see a long tradition behind him and appreciate how he adopts old methods to new uses.

Many early lays must have told of single combats. The type survives in Homer, and we can see what the archetypal form was. The combatants meet, and we may be told something about one or the other. The first throws his spear and probably misses; the second throws *his* spear and does better in that he hits his opponent's armour. But at this point the opponent rallies and kills him. This simple form can be worked into sequences either of Achaean and Trojan victories or of a single man's career on the battlefield. But though this is a fundamental form, Homer is highly ingenious in varying it. No two of his battle-scenes are exactly alike; a man may be killed in one line or in fifty. The Homeric *aristeia*, in which a single hero performs in succession a number of feats and wins a number of victories, is in fact a multiplied version of the original single combat, and it gains its interest from the variety of persons and blows and wounds which Homer gives to it.

A common theme in heroic poetry is when two warriors meet on the battlefield and, after exchanging words, fight. Such is the basis of two famous episodes, the Old High German meeting of Hildebrand and Hadibrand and the Persian meeting of Sohrab and Rustum. These are famous because in both a father encounters his son without knowing it and kills him. Homer has no parallel to this tragic theme, but he knows the device and uses it with skill and invention. In both cases he plunges into the middle of affairs, and in both he devises an unexpected ending. At xx 156 ff., in the general turmoil of battle, two great warriors meet, eager to fight. They are Aeneas and Achilles. Achilles speaks first in sharp and taunting words and tells his opponent to retire to the ranks and give up the idea of fighting him. Both are the sons of goddesses, and Aeneas is not put off by Achilles' overpowering manner. He boasts of his own ancestry and then, in a vivid simile, deplores the rude words of Achilles and his way of treating an opponent:

'But what need is there that we should exchange strife and abuse against each other, like women who grow angry in a heart-eating quarrel and go into the middle of the street and abuse each other with words true and false; for these also does anger command'. (xx 251-5)

After this they fight, and the fight is reported in some detail with an eye for surprise and variety. Aeneas acquits himself as well in battle as in words, but then the gods end the struggle by setting a mist on the eyes of Achilles and spiriting Aeneas away from the battlefield. This is a full treatment of a traditional theme and is not only thrilling in itself but adds important touches to the personalities of both Achilles and Aeneas. The episode is in the short traditional style, but has a secondary importance in the career of Achilles.

A more surprising example of this device comes at vi 119-236. Glaucus and Diomedes meet in battle, and Diomedes asks Glaucus who he is. Glaucus replies with the tale of his ancestor Bellerophon who came to Lycia and fought the Chimaera. Diomedes, learning that he is of Greek origin, welcomes him as a family friend. Fighting is out of the question, and the two warriors clasp hands and give pledges. Then Homer ends the episode:

Then Zeus, son of Cronus, robbed Glaucus of his wits, for he exchanged with Diomedes golden armour for bronze, a hundred oxen's worth for what was worth nine. (vi 234-6)

This is delightfully unforeseen. Homer often laughs at the gods but hardly ever at heroes, but the laugh is to the credit of Glaucus, who is carried away by generosity. An old device is given an entirely new character, which surprisingly fits into the battle by providing a moment of delightful relaxation.

Traces of short lays are visible at many places in the *Iliad*. Though the present division into twenty-four books may be the work of Alexandrian scholars, it follows natural breaks in the narrative and the portions so divided often have the appearance of complete poems. Some of them were certainly recited in isolation in antiquity, and it is likely that short poems of this kind existed before Homer and may even have been composed by him in his formative years. The art of the short lay is marked and tenacious, and has its own elegances. Book i, which starts the *Iliad*, is a rich and rounded poem, with fine contrasts of temper and action, high passions and exalted eloquence; it begins with a crisis and ends with the gods going to sleep on Olympus. Many other books of the *Iliad* are equally well constructed, and it is easy to believe that Homer intended to give them their own kind of unity. There is a like balance in Books viii, x, xi, xvi, xxii, xxiii and xxiv. The shield of Achilles in xviii can be read as a complete poem; Books iii–v form a longer unity; Book ix, despite its richly worked material, begins in a crisis and ends in gloom. The whole career of Achilles, from when he takes the field in xix to the death of Hector in xxii, has the air of a small epic, even if it has been enriched with not entirely relevant additions. Throughout the *Iliad* we can see how construction on a small scale gives life to the separate parts, and this life is essentially that of the short lay.

At the same time the short lays are not detached from the whole poem but worked into it with care and skill. They have their unobtrusive references to passages outside their own immediate scope but worked into the main pattern. For instance, though Achilles is absent from the battlefield for a very long period, he is brought to mind at intervals in an unobtrusive but effective way. The wrath, which is accountable for the Achaean reverses, is mentioned at various points by Apollo (iv 512), Hera (v 788), Agamemnon (vii 113), Nestor (xi 664), the poet himself (xii 10), and Poseidon (xiv 366). The poet holds his events together by this thread until the climax comes when Patroclus goes to battle and after his death Achilles dominates the poem. In a rather similar way the preeminence of Achilles is kept before us by occasional references to him and his exploits. Andromache reminds Hector that Achilles killed her father but gave him honourable burial (vi 414 ff.), and also her seven brothers. He captured Priam's sons, Isos and Antiphus, and sold them for ransom (xi 104–6), but they were killed later by Agamemnon. Hecamede, who works for Nestor, was captured by Achilles when he took Tenedos (xi 625). The separate episodes, in which Achilles has no part, are held together by these passing references which keep him in mind.

Once Homer had decided to construct a long poem and to use for it episodes which may have provided matter for short poems he shaped some of its parts with their technique, but the *Iliad* has more than this. The various portions are brought together in a main design, and inside this Homer enriches the story with passages which bear little relation to short poems but fit very well into his Iliad. To keep his poem full and varied he takes advantage of certain places to add a whole chapter of events. For instance, when the duel between Hector and Aias has proved inconclusive, the next day sees a general conflict in many fields and this is the matter of Book viii. When Patroclus is killed, Achilles does not hear of it at once, but for the whole of Book xvii fighting takes place over the dead man's body. These long stretches of narrative help to make the poem an Iliad. They are not in themselves very shapely, but they make a serious contribution to the poem by spreading its scope and at the same time delaying any final action until we are really ready for it. When Achilles is told of the death of Patroclus, the long delay whets our interest and makes his preeminence more insistent.

The duel between two warriors could be more than a mere duel. If the contest was between two sufficiently important people, the whole plot might turn on it. This is the case with the duel between Paris and Menelaus in Book iii. By abducting Helen, Paris provoked Menelaus to unite the Achaeans in war against Troy. A fight between the two heroes could solve the whole problem. It does not, because, when Paris is on the verge of defeat and death, Aphrodite rescues him. The war then starts again in earnest. We might think that this was sufficient for this subject, and it is surprising that in Book vii there is another duel between Hector and Aias, where no question arises of either being responsible for the war. They fight by right of their heroic preeminence. Hector is the bravest Trojan, and Aias, though chosen by lot, is the bravest Achaean after Achilles (ii 768). This duel is a real trial of strength, but, like the first duel, it ends inconclusively, by night falling and putting an end to fighting. We may assume that in the many tales told about Troy such duels had a place and though that between Paris and Menelaus held pride of place, there must have been others. Homer seems to feel that he can use two, and he takes care to make them quite different, in both their cause and their course. The character of both, and equally the absence of Achilles from them, help to swell the poem to an Iliad.

The plot of the *Odyssey* is less episodic and more complex than that of the *Iliad*. The first four books tell what is happening in Ithaca in the absence of Odysseus, especially to the young Telemachus, who seeks news on a journey, but their interest is less as a separable tale than as a preparation for the return of Odysseus and his vengeance on the Suitors. The poet is at home with a long poem and able to exploit its possibilities. Nor are the adventures of Odysseus on his way from Calypso's island self-contained units; they lead through a series of crises to his arrival on Phaeacia. Then follows his reception at the court and his ultimate revelation of himself. But once Odysseus begins to tell his own story the technique changes. He relates a series of adventures simply by their sequence in time and by the gradual loss of men and ships until Odysseus alone survives. The subjects must have been told many times and each could have fallen easily into the limits of a short lay.

The scale of these episodes varies greatly. On the one side are those which are despatched in a very few lines—the attack on Ismarus (22), the Lotus-eaters (22), Aeolus (76), the Laestrygonians (52), the Sirens (46), Scylla and Charybdis (38). On the other hand three are on a full scale—the Cyclops (461), Circe (241), and the summoning of ghosts at the end of the world (640), though of this substantial parts may be later additions. Half-way comes the eating of the cattle of the sun (130), with its consequences in the loss of Odysseus' ship and companions. This difference of scale corresponds with living practice in short lays, which varies enormously and offers poems as short as Homer's shortest episodes and longer than his longest. Yet there is no defect of art in the variation of scale. If more were said about the Laestrygonians, they would impinge on the Cyclops, whose habits they share; if more were said about the Lotus Eaters, it would be a surfeit of a kind of poetry which must not last too long. But the Cyclops deserves all that he can get, for he subsumes at least three ancient, world-wide stories, the trick of the name 'No-Man', the blinding of the one-eyed giant, and the escape under the sheep. Circe provides all the thrill of an enchantress, but also forecasts the future to Odysseus. The scene with the ghosts is highly dramatic and imaginative and demands space for its present interest and its importance for the future of Odysseus. In his discrimination between the claims of different stories Homer is in full command of his material.

The second half of the *Odyssey* is hardly episodic at all. Once Odysseus lands in Ithaca his adventures are indeed complex but they follow a single line of development, which ends in the slaughter of the Suitors and his recognition by Penelope. This may have been in part enforced on him by having to deal with three separate persons or groups of persons, Odysseus himself, his son Telemachus, and Penelope and the Suitors. In the end all three converge, but to keep them fully at work the episodic method would be less effective than a continuous narrative which shifts from one group to another. This looks like an advance on the episodic method. The various stages, such as the different recognitions of Odysseus, are an ascending series, beginning with Telemachus and ending with Penelope, not separate enclosed events. Each takes him nearer to his goal. It is true that when Odysseus is recognized by his old dog Argos the scene has a beautiful development and shape, but it is none the less one of a sequence. Again, when the seer Theoclymenus sees the Suitors threatened with a deadly doom (20.351 ff.), it is splendid in its brief compass, but it belongs to the vengeance of Odysseus which is not far away. If the *Iliad* shows many signs of the short lay and its techniques, the *Odyssey*, in its second half, seems to have broken away from this and to be experimenting with continuous narrative. This change of technique throws no light on the problem of authorship; for it could be explained equally by a poet who changed his manner as he grew older and by a second poet who, being trained differently from the older generation, was more at home with a long poem.

The episodic manner of construction demands that an episode, once completed, must manifestly be seen to be so. At the same time there must be adequate means of starting afresh after it. Homer does this in his own way. The highly dramatic Book i ends with the gods going to sleep in their separate dwellings, among them Zeus with Hera (i 609–11). Then Book ii begins with a renewal of action, and what better way than to start by saying that, while men and gods slept, Zeus alone did not (ii 1–2)? This may be a formal contradiction but that makes it all the better, and the story continues with a new initiative taken by Zeus. Book viii ends with a scene of calm beauty as the Trojan watch-fires burn on the plain; Book ix begins with a powerful contrast, as the Achaeans, smitten almost with panic, meet in the tent of Agamemnon and discuss how to get Achilles back into the battle. When these negotiations break down and Achilles remains unmoved, a deep gloom settles on the Achaean leaders, but Book x takes advantage of it by a contrasting adventure of night-operations, lurid and harsh and brutal. Each of the last three books of the *Iliad* is in some degree self-contained, and has its theme and tone, in the last fight between Achilles and Hector, the funeral games of Patroclus, and the ransom of Hector's body by Priam from Achilles. But each fits into the main scheme and contributes something indispensable to it.

Though most of the *Odyssey* moves either in a series of almost unconnected episodes or in a closely woven tale, at one point the poet takes what looks like a big risk. Books 1–4 have told of Telemachus' voyage in search of news of Odysseus, and so far Odysseus, though often mentioned, has not been introduced directly. But Book 5 opens a whole new movement and starts

with a real crux. In Book 1 the gods in council decide that
Odysseus shall come home, and to further this Hermes is to be
sent to Calypso to tell her to release him, while Athene herself will
go to Ithaca. The second part of the policy is then put into action.
At the beginning of Book 5 we hear again of a council on Olympus,
which decides to send Hermes to Calypso. If this is the same council, as it seems to be, we may ask why so much is repeated; if it is
not the same council, but a second one, why is it so like the first,
and why is it needed? The only solution must be found in the
needs of composition. The second council exists in case the reciter
wishes to start his tale at this point, omitting the previous interesting but detachable books about Telemachus, and therefore plunges
afresh into what is really a repetition of what has already been said
but with the emphasis now on the actual return of Odysseus
rather than on Athene's visit to Ithaca. This second opening
could have been made by the original poet and used as an alternative start, or it could have been made by some disciple who recited
the poems and adapted them in this way to suit the time at his
disposal or the demands of his audience.

A trouble with long oral poems is that they have no easy or
ready way of dealing with simultaneous actions. In the short lay
this does not matter, since its normal line of advance is from one
incident to another. In the *Iliad* this still dominates the development, but we must make some reservations about it. We assume
that on the battlefield one fight follows another, and that on the
few occasions where simultaneous actions take place, it is to avoid
boredom by presenting a more agreeable alternative. But on the
battlefield this does not happen. There are indeed happy variants
like the meeting of Diomedes and Glaucus, but most of the battle
seems to consist of separate encounters, one following another in
sequence. Yet we may be wrong to assume this. At xi 84 we hear
'as long as it was morning and the holy day waxed' and then much
later as xvi 777 'as long as the sun bestrode the centre of heaven'.
Now in the interval a very great deal has happened, and yet, it
seems, only a few hours have passed. The solution of course is that
Homer is not very interested in a time table, but likes to keep

each episode clear and clean. There was no means by which he could arrange his events in a chronological order, still less in a geographical scheme giving different parts of the battlefield. Yet this is what he suggests. These events all take place, not necessarily in exact sequence or in the same place. In short lays no problem arises, and in long poems there is a problem only if we wish to create it.

The *Odyssey* deals with a somewhat different problem. It has in its first half two main subjects, the return of Odysseus and the situation of Ithaca, which is combined with the voyage of Telemachus to Pylos and Sparta. The poet deals with this in a simple way. The first four books handle Telemachus and Ithaca, the next eight Odysseus. In Book 13 the two threads begin to converge when Odysseus arrives on Ithaca, and they do so completely when Odysseus and Telemachus meet at the hut of Eumaeus (16.1 ff.). To make this easy Homer courageously leaves the main line of his story when Odysseus is with Eumaeus and shifts back to Telemachus whose departure from Pylos and return to Ithaca is told at some length (15.1–300). This looks like a novelty, demanded by the needs of a full-scale narrative with a complex plot, and on the whole the poet manages it very well, mainly because he keeps its salient points simple. When at 15.301 he turns back to Odysseus he says simply: 'But in the hut, Odysseus and good Eumaeus took their supper . . .' There are of course other simultaneous happenings, but they are not very troublesome. For instance, while Odysseus is sleeping in a bush after arriving on Phaeacia, Athene sets Nausicaa to find him (5.491–3; 6.1 ff.). Again, after Telemachus has landed safely, his ship sails to the city, and the Suitors are foiled in their plan to kill him (16.342–448). This is a more ambitious art than the detached scenes in the *Iliad* and suggests that the poet is finding confidence in a new kind of composition.

The poet's sense of unity and design is well exemplified by his skill in weaving a set of stories into a single whole. Odysseus is a hero of folk-tale, and many stories are told about him. To tell these episodically would be shapeless and commonplace; the poet makes Odysseus tell them himself and so not only gives them a sequence but makes them reflect the hero's own personality. Books 9 to 12 contain his own story. This technique is not unique in such poetry. In the Assyrian version of *Gilgamesh*, when the hero sails to the end of the world he meets Uta-Napishtim, the old Semitic prototype of Noah, who tells him at some length of the flood and how he himself, who survived it, has been made immortal. This fits well into the plan of the poem, which is largely taken up with the designs of Gilgamesh to escape death. Uta-Napishtim speaks with authority on a central theme and his story explains its significance. In the Ainu epic *Kulune Shirka*, which amounts to some 4000 lines, the hero tells the story himself and speaks from his own point of view. Since the story has shamanistic elements, it is possible that the bard is a shaman who enacts a part and speaks for it. Yet this need not always be the case. In the vast Kirghiz epic of Manas, in one version a substantial part of the story is put in the mouth of the hero Alaman Bet, and this adds much to the variety of the poem by telling it from a different point of view and allowing a hero to give his thoughts and emotions more personally than an impartial poet can for him.

This method has obvious dramatic advantages, but it also presents some difficulties. When the poet tells the tale in the third person, he is presumed to know everything, and we take his word for it, but when an actor in the story speaks, he is limited by his own knowledge. This does not much matter, and Homer usually gets round it. For instance when Odysseus says that Zeus sends a storm (9.67), it is a perfectly natural thing to think. When he more emphatically says that Zeus disregards a sacrifice and intends to destroy Odysseus' companians and ships (9.553–5), this is a conclusion made with after-knowledge. Yet, just as in the author's narrative certain things are implied or taken for granted, so they are in the narrative of Odysseus. When he is sailing from the island of Aeolus and is almost within sight of Ithaca, he falls asleep, and his companions plot to seize the bag, which contains the winds, but which they think to contain treasure (10.31–45). Odysseus, telling the tale, repeats their actual words, which he cannot have heard, but which are necessary to the story. Again, when he sets out alone on Circe's island to rescue his companions whom she has turned into beasts, he meets a handsome young man who tells how to defeat Circe and get his companions restored to human shape (10.277 ff.). This young man, as Odysseus says, is Hermes, but he has no means of knowing that he is, since Hermes does not disclose his identity. He is necessary to the story, and that is enough. Finally, the last catastrophe is caused by the eating of the cattle of the Sun when Odysseus is again asleep, and here too Odysseus reports a speech in twelve lines (12.340–51) by Eurylochus, which he cannot have heard. These small slips or tricks need not trouble us, but Homer may perhaps have been a little uneasy about them, as we can see from this same episode when Odysseus says that he learned the facts from Calypso, who learned it from Hermes, who learned it from the nymph Lampetie (12.374–90). This exception is not a success, and we can understand that Homer usually preferred to exercise a little legerdemain in allowing special knowledge to Odysseus.

An advantage of the long poem is that it can incidentally introduce subsidiary themes which may not be very closely connected with its main subject but none the less enrich it. This was easy for a poet brought up on a large number of stories from which he could pick what he wished. Such stories may sometimes be exemplary, as when Phoenix tells of the anger of Meleager and its disastrous consequences, hoping that it may persuade Achilles to abate his own (ix 527–99). In a less direct way Nestor's reminiscences of his youth (i 254–84) are aimed at abating the hatred between Achilles and Agamemnon. But more usually such incidental stories are told for their own sake. Glaucus' account of his ancestor Bellerophon (vi 150–211) to Diomedes not only wins him a friend but conveys his high lineage and his inborn nobility. When Eumaeus tells Odysseus of his childhood when he was sold by a treacherous nurse to Phoenician traders (15.403–84), there is much charm and pathos and drama which lie outside the scope of the main story. Such tales may not be wholly necessary, but this one confirms our high opinion of Eumaeus, who is now a slave

but was born a prince and keeps his inborn nobility. In a somewhat different way Homer tells a tale to provide a background to
some incident in his story. Odysseus has a scar on his leg, and it is
one of the signs by which the returned wanderer is known. The
poet tells at some length how Odysseus got it in a boar hunt
(19.392–467). A special variation on this device are the two lying
stories which Odysseus tells first to Eumaeus (14.192–359) and
later to Antinous (17.419–44). They vary in detail and in scale,
but both give a picture of Achaeans making piratical raids on
Egypt and fighting and looting there, usually with loss to the
Achaeans. This looks very like an ancient memory of the days of
the Sea Raiders in the thirteenth and twelfth centuries, when
Aegean peoples attacked Egypt in force. Odysseus lies boldly and
circumstantially, but his lies gain in strength because they are
based on a genuine historical tradition.

Though in many ways Homer uses the art of the short heroic
lay whose very nature dictates certain habits to it, he also at times
betrays his attempt to deal with events on a larger scale and to
shape them into a more comprehensive pattern. It looks as if in his
day the long poem was exceptional and had to make use of the art
of the short poem, which indeed was useful up to a point but then
called for some management and adaptation. The development of
an ancient technique for new purposes matches other characteristics of Homeric poetry. In this respect also, Homeric art is very far
from being fossilized by convention.

CHAPTER FIVE

The Greek Heroic Age

MANY peoples cherish the legend of an age which, in the splendour and the scope of its achievements and in the prodigious
qualities of the men who took part in them, is thought to eclipse
all that come after it. The Greek belief in such an age appears in
Hesiod's account of the decline of mankind through four ages,
Golden, Silver, Bronze, and Iron, where an age of Heroes appears
between the last two, and though it spoils the sequence, is clearly
important:

Now when this race also was hidden by the earth, Zeus son of Cronos
created yet another, a fourth, on the bounteous earth, juster and better,
a divine race of heroes, who are called demi-gods, the earlier race upon
the boundless earth. They were killed by evil war and terrible battle,
some at seven-gated Thebes, the land of Cadmus, fighting for the flocks
of Oedipus' son; others were brought in ships over the great gulf of the
sea to Troy for the sake of Helen of the beautiful hair. (*Works and
Days* 156–65)

Though the word *hērōs* originally meant no more than warrior, it
came to assume more august associations and to imply a special
superiority in human endowments and endeavours. Hence the
Greeks believed in a heroic age, in which men were sons of gods,
and spent themselves in two great wars, the war of the Seven
against Thebes and the siege of Troy. Though the first of these
made large contributions to legend and provided matter for
tragedies in the fifth century, the second was even more dominating, largely because it provides the whole setting of the *Iliad* and
is presupposed in the *Odyssey*. These are heroic poems because
they tell of heroes, and these heroes are placed in a heroic age,

whose members were not 'such as men now are' (v 304; xii 449; xx 287). They have an aura of grandeur and consort with gods.

Most heroic ages have a foundation in historical reality. The Germanic peoples found theirs in the vast movements and changes of the fourth to the sixth century; the Russians in the twelfth century in the time of Vladimir Monomakh of Kiev (1113–25); the Serbs round the battle of Kosovo in 1389, when the old Serbian kingdom was destroyed by the Turks; the French round the wars of Charlemagne against the Saracens. Such cycles of legend are not history. They are packed with inventions, distortions and omissions; they place events in their own, often false perspective; they disregard boundaries of space and time and bring persons of quite different generations together on a single stage. Even the central real event round which a legend clusters need not be of any lasting importance. Roland was indeed killed at Roncesvalles in 788, but it was in an insignificant skirmish, fought not against Saracens but against Basques. Nor need a leading character, like Beowulf or Sigurth, necessarily have existed. Heroic legend is not history, but in many societies it takes the place of history and must be treated on its merits as an artistic resurrection of the past. To see it correctly we must find what lies behind it, and how its special manifestations came into existence.

The belief in a heroic age is not universal, nor are the conditions in which it is born always the same. We can discern several ways in which it can emerge. The first is among peoples who have been conquered and console themselves for lost grandeur by exalting the past to a special glory. Such a feeling fostered the beliefs of the Welsh under their Anglo-Saxon and Norman conquerors, and of the Russians after their annihilating defeat by the Mongols at the battle of the Kalka in 1228. A second cause is when a people leaves home for some distant land and keeps touch with its past by glorifying it in legends. This has happened with the Norsemen in Iceland and Greenland, and with the Maoris in New Zealand. While the first look back to the crowded days of Attila, Ermanaric and Theodoric, the second look back to the incredible voyages which brought their ancestors in canoes 2000 miles over open sea.

A third cause is when a political system disintegrates, and success and dominion give place to dissolution and decay. This happens after the death of Charlemagne, whose reign in retrospect is seen to be of heroic resplendence. The Greek belief in a heroic age may have been formed from two causes. An actual age of remarkable distinction existed in the thirteenth century B.C. and was afire with energy and effort. This came to a violent, if not a sudden, end, and its memory was carried overseas by the mainland Greeks who colonized Ionia from about 1100 onwards. It was their bond with the past, treasured and cherished as an heirloom. It fostered their most precious possession in the living art of song, and though the Trojan War was by no means its only theme, it was certainly preeminent.

We can hardly doubt that the Trojan War was a historical fact. Throughout antiquity the site of Troy was identified, with a hillock, now known as Hisarlik, on the Asiatic shore near the sea some ten miles south of Cape Helles. The site was excavated in 1870 by Heinrich Schliemann, who unearthed a series of cities built one on the other from about 3000. For two thousand years the site had an almost uninterrupted career, varied by occasional disasters from earthquake and fire. The cities known as VI and VIIa fit the legends of Troy as Homer tells them. VIIa was destroyed at some date, not yet fixed precisely, in the middle of the thirteenth century, and this suits the date which Herodotus gives, about eight hundred years before himself (2.145.4), i.e. about 1240. The city was burned and probably looted. It confirms the legend and gives a historical basis to it.

The excavations at Troy have been followed by many others in Aegean lands, and abundant evidence testifies to a rich and highly organized society first in Crete, where its heyday was from 1700 to about 1400, then on the mainland from 1600 to 1200 notably at Mycenae, Tiryns and Pylos, though many other sites have yielded remains. The civilization of 'Minoan' Crete, called after the legendary king Minos, was almost certainly not Greek but possibly derived from Asia Minor; the civilization of 'Mycenaean' Greece, called after its most impressive site, was certainly

Greek, at least in its later phases. It grew out of the Minoan culture,
and it seems that about 1400 the Greeks invaded Crete and took
over its places and palaces, without reviving its former glories.
Power was now based on the mainland, with Mycenae as a possible
centre. The new culture resembled the old but made significant
changes. Above all it was organized for war. Mycenaean cities had
Cyclopean stone walls, massive gateways and protecting towers.
Though Troy had relations with this society, it was not part of it
and remained culturally separate and distinct. Mycenae was
remarkably rich, and its graves have yielded much fine gold-work.
We do not know the sources of this wealth but surmise that loot
in war may have been one and the export of fine wares and
luxuries another.

Some information of Aegean politics between 1400 and 1200
can be gathered from the Hittite records, discovered in the royal
archives at Boghaz-Köy, the ancient Hattusas, in central Anatolia.
At this time the Hittites controlled a large part of Asia Minor, and
among other countries were in contact with one called Ahhijawā,
in which we may recognize the historical prototype of Achaea,
the country of Homer's Achaeans. Since its king is more than
once mentioned, sometimes with respect, it must have been of
some importance. Its people are busy on the western and southern
coasts of Asia Minor, first as allies or friends of the Hittites, later,
as the Hittite empire is shaken within and without, as adversaries.
The documents even preserve some names of the Ahhijawā
commanders, but none can be identified with any Greek known to
us. In the middle of the thirteenth century the Hittites were faced
by a dangerous revolt on their western sea-board led by the
people of Arzawa, but it is not clear that the Achaeans took part
on either side. Among the enemies of the Hittites the documents
mention a place, Taruisa, which may be Troy. The Hittite king
claims that he vanquished the rebels, but we do not know how
successful he was. Though the Achaeans are not mentioned, it
is possible that they took advantage of Troy being weakened, and
attacked it. The thirteenth century was a time of such far-spread
activity that the Trojan War falls easily into it. Even so, though

Troy was certainly burned, we cannot be certain that it was burned by Achaeans. No contemporary documents say so, and legend is prone to falsify. But at the least the Achaeans, with strong bases on the mainland and advanced posts on the Asiatic coast, were well placed for large expeditions oversea. Their motive may have been loot. Troy was a rich city, and its sack would be rewarding. But they may also have wished to break into Asia Minor at a time when Hittite control was shaken. If so, they did not realize their aim.

Legend, busy in the living art of poetry, attributed to the glorious past warriors whose names were common at all times, but are now known from the Mycenaean tablets of Pylos to have been current about 1200. Though the Mycenaean script is so incompetent that each name can be read in more than one way, some names at least are the same as occur in the epic, and in all some sixty may be. Of these very few belong to important figures in Homer. The main exception is A-ki-reu, which may be Akhilleus, i.e. Achilles, and appears both at Knossos and Pylos for men of no importance. More remarkable is that among these names twenty are those of warriors fighting on the Trojan side and include not only Glaucus and Pandarus but Hector (E-ko-to), who holds small plots of land at Pylos. It seems unlikely that historical Trojans had Greek names, and, though we cannot rule out the possibility that the Greeks adapted Trojan names to Greek forms as they may have adapted the Hittite Alaksandus to Alexandros, an alternative name for Paris, it is more likely that they followed a common custom of bards who tell of foreign peoples, and attached names from their own language to imaginary foreign characters. Hector is so canonized as the chief Trojan that we shrink from thinking that he is an invention. But his place in the *Iliad* suggests that the poets have done much for him, and his name, 'holder', is well fitted to him as the 'prop' of Troy, 'for Hector alone protected Ilios' (vi 403). These Mycenaean names prove nothing for history, except that the poets gave their characters actual and familiar names, which may be of considerable antiquity.

We cannot but ask why the Trojan War gained so prominent a place in legend. An explanation may perhaps be found in what happened after its end. It seems to have weakened the Achaean power. This is what legend says, and in his own way the Hittite king confirms it by his reduced respect for the Achaeans in the thirteenth century. Moreover, some fifty years or so after the war the Mycenaean empire, if such it was, and certainly the Mycenaean civilization, collapsed. This seems to have been the work of rude invaders from the north-west, who were later known as Dorians and were Greeks of a kind. The great palaces were burned, the fine arts ceased to have craftsmen or patrons. Above all, the special script which the Mycenaeans used for their official documents, and which was devised for specialist scribes, disappeared, and Greece remained illiterate until a new, alphabetic writing came into use about 750. This alone testifies to an enormous catastrophe, but other evidence confirms it. The Mycenaeans held out for a time at Mycenae and longer at Athens. Elsewhere they were dispossessed, except for those who escaped across the sea to found colonies. No doubt songs had already been composed about the great doings at Troy and passed into the repertory of bards. When the catastrophe came, these songs, which may have begun as praises of the living or laments for the dead, began to celebrate the past as a uniquely glorious age. When, possibly from Pylos by way of Athens, Greek colonists moved to Ionia and colonized Smyrna and other places *c.* 1100, they brought the art of song with them and treasured it as their most binding link with the homeland and the glittering past. In due course the living tradition produced the Homeric poems, which through it reached back to Mycenaean days and forward to the new age which came with the revival of writing and the awakening of Ionia in the eighth century.

This heroic age, as the Greek imagination shaped it, lasted for not more than four generations, of which the last was the generation of those who fought at Troy. This suits the collapse of the Mycenaean world about 1200. The beginning is obscure, but so it usually is for such ages; and it may mean that ancestries were lost in the turmoil of events and human forbears conveniently replaced by gods. The divine descent of heroes accounts for their heroism and would be agreeable to princes who claimed descent from them and were proud to hear such achievements told in song. The close kinship between men and gods is a sign of the high splendour of the men, but it may also reflect an ancient poetical art which sang of both gods and men and found satisfaction in bringing them together. Once a tradition had begun to form it was natural that tales originally distinct and separate should be combined into a wonderfully various body of saga. Hesiod shows that the Trojan War was a central point in this, but he gives equal prominence to the war of the Seven against Thebes. This is known to the *Iliad*, where Diomedes tells Agamemnon that his generation is better than its fathers (iv 405). This second war against Thebes belongs to the immediate past, and Diomedes took part in it. Its importance may have been dimmed by that of Troy, and it may have been remembered more for its single exploits than for its general consequences. That the Achaeans should pass from a local war to a foreign was in accord with their restless spirit. The tale of Thebes provided matter for many poems, and in antiquity a *Thebaid* was attributed by some to Homer but denied to him by others. It seems to have lacked the Homeric coherence, but that did not prevent its episodes from being lurid and popular.

Hesiod regards the Trojan War as a capital event and climax of the heroic age. In this he may have reflected fact, but legend is not always just in its decisions on such a matter. The fight at Roncesvalles, which informs the *Song of Roland*, was in fact a trivial affair; the mutual slaughter of Burgundians and Huns in the *Elder Edda* took place on the battlefield and not at the court of Attila; the Russian heroes of Kiev seem in legend to have no adversaries comparable to their actual enemies the Mongols. If analogy were a sure guide, we could argue that the Trojan War may well have taken place but was probably not of much importance. On the other hand analogy sometimes presents solid counterparts for legend. The Serbian defeat at Kosovo was a total catastrophe, and the ruins of Troy suggest that something annihilating happened. Even so we must ask why Greek imagination selected the war of Troy, when there were surely many other notable themes in the fourteenth and thirteenth centuries. One possible answer is that the Trojan War may have been the effort of a united Greece such as did not occur again till Alexander. A coalition on this scale may have impressed the disunited Greeks of subsequent generations as something indeed wonderful. On the other hand the siege of Troy may have won pride of place because it was not only the greatest but the last achievement of the Mycenaean Greeks. After it they never did anything on the same scale, and it is possible that their decline began soon after the capture. In that case the Trojan War has the appeal of an event in which a people is indeed victorious but so exhausts itself in victory that this is its last achievement. A later generation, living in exile from its first home, might well see such a war as possessing a tragic grandeur and worthy of celebration in song.

The Greek heroic age has been compared with other such ages in one special respect. Just as the chief figures in it are the high king Agamemnon and a few prominent leaders round him, so elsewhere the *dramatis personae* are often the king, who is *primus inter pares*, and his peers or comrades, who work with him and are only a little short of him in authority. This is the case in Germanic poetry, including Norse and Anglo-Saxon, and also in French, Russian and Jugoslav, but it would be wrong to see in these the reflection of a feudal order. The heroic order is much simpler and is meant for war; the king shares the work with his captains, who are themselves eminent in the field. The same thing happens in the Mongol and Tatar epics, where the great leader is surrounded by other warriors who have their own exploits and win their own glory. No doubt legend and poetry simplify the facts, but the facts seem real enough. If there was a Greek force that attacked Troy, it would almost certainly be a coalition, and a coalition demands both a commander-in-chief and a manageable number of other commanders under him. These are brought together in a single, large undertaking, but if this is lacking, they perform their exploits by themselves, and the body of legends is a cycle of their doings. This is very much the case with the Russians, where Vladimir is indeed king but is not himself very forceful, while his princes go out and fight monsters and outlaws.

21. *Excavations have revealed that the houses and walls of Troy VIIa were destroyed by fire, and that large storage jars were sunk beneath the floors, suggesting preparations for a siege—strong evidence that this was the Homeric Troy (see p. 81)*

22. LEFT: *The 'Great Casemate' inside one of the Cyclopean walls of Tiryns,* C. *1200* B.C. *(see p. 21)*

23. *The gold death mask* ABOVE *from Mycenae was thought by Schliemann to represent the face of Agamemnon. In fact it dates from about 1500* B.C., *many generations before the time of the king*

24. *The two gold cups from Vaphio show scenes in the capture of a wild bull, first in a net, then by means of a decoy cow*
25. *A gold diadem, sixteenth century also from Mycenae*

If prowess and success in war provide a central principle for a heroic age, and its chief aim is glory, yet glory calls to be displayed in visible forms and heroism is marked by external trappings in wealth beyond the dreams of later generations. The Greek heroic age was believed to have been incalculably rich, and this is natural when it is seen in retrospect by an impoverished posterity, but for it there is a solid basis in fact, as the rich discoveries of gold-work in sites such as Mycenae show. This echoes in the epithet 'rich in gold' applied to Mycenae (3.304) and more vaguely but no less forcibly by the impression made on Telemachus and the young Peisistratus by the palace of Menelaus at Sparta:

There was a gleam as of the sun or the moon in the high-roofed hall of glorious Menelaus. (4.45–6)

and Telemachus comments:

'Look at the light flashing in the echoing halls of bronze, and gold and electrum and silver and ivory.' (4. 71–3)

Those masterpieces of Mycenaean gold-work, the Vaphio cups, came from this part of Greece and in their small way justify the legend.

Memories of the glorious past are more brilliantly magnified for the palace of Alcinous in Phaeacia, which lies on the edge of fairy-land but still catches light from the Mycenaean past. The doors are of gold with silver posts and bronze lintels, and on either side are gold and silver dogs made by Hephaestus to act as sentries (7.84 ff.). Gold is a sign of heroic wealth. The armour of Glaucus is made of gold (vi 236); the staff of Achilles (i 246) has gold studs, presumably on its handle; the cuirass of Agamemnon is made of gold, tin and blue enamel (xi 25–7), and comes from Cyprus, which suggests the wide spread of heroic society. Much more significant is the armour which Hephaestus makes for Achilles (xviii 478–613), where the shield, adorned with scenes of peace and war, recalls to some degree the art of daggers found at Mycenae and combining gold, silver, tin and enamel. The technique is not quite accurately reported and we need not assume that the poet ever saw such a shield, but tradition must have told something about this art, and it is possible that in the Mycenaean heyday works of such costly accomplishment were actually made. Their memory survived in some form, and as Homer tells of the shield, it is the work of a god but for that reason all the more appropriate to a great hero.

Heroic societies are commonly on the move in their quest for adventure and booty, and the Achaeans were no exception. They seem indeed to have penetrated where later Greeks did not for some centuries, and echoes of their travels survived in song. Perhaps the most striking in the *Iliad* is the account given by Achilles of Egyptian Thebes with its great wealth and its hundred gates, each with its two hundred men and chariots (ix 381–4). The wealth recalls the temple built by Amenhotep III (1411–1376 B.C.) with its floors and doors of gold and silver; the hundred gates are a Greek version of his many pylons; the exploits of his troops were recorded in inscriptions which survived to much later days. Similar memories of Egyptian wealth may be seen in the gifts, including two silver baths, which Menelaus and Helen receive from their hosts in Thebes (4.125 ff.). In contrast with Egypt the Hittite Empire hardly makes a showing. A possible mention of Hittites is a passing reference to the ghost of Achilles by Odysseus about Neoptolemus killing people called Keteioi, who may be Hittites (11.521), but the reference is uncertain, and bears little relation to the main story. In the thirteenth century the Achaeans had to reckon with the Hittites, but Greek legend says nothing of them but concentrates on the small city of Troy which lay on the north-western corner of their empire.

History, as we know it from the Hittite records, suggests that the Achaeans were a military monarchy under a king. Of course he may have had other kings under him, and his suzerainty may have been based on a confederacy. We assume that he ruled from Mycenae, but he is likely to have had an advanced stronghold in some such place as Rhodes, within striking distance of the Asiatic coast. The Achaean king finds his literary counterpart in Agamemnon, who rules 'over many islands and all Argos' (ii 108), where even if Argos is restricted to the Peloponnese or a part of it, the dominion is still large. In the Homeric poems Agamemnon is commander-in-chief, and we presume that his power is specifically for war. This may not be far from historical fact, and the special prominence of Agamemnon may explain why a Hittite king calls the king of Ahhiyawā 'brother'.

Though Greek heroic poetry seems to have been rooted in the Mycenaean past and to preserve certain notable characteristics of its power and wealth, we must not expect much precise information from it or trust all that it says. Parallels from elsewhere suggest that small pieces of truth are mixed up with large quantities of fancy, and there is no sure way of telling which is which unless we have external evidence of quite a different nature. But in one place it is possible that the *Iliad* contains a political or historical document. At ii 484–760 survives the Catalogue of the Achaean ships, purporting to be a list of the Achaean contingents with the names of their leaders and the number of their ships.

At the start it is clear that this is not the work of the poet of the *Iliad* but incorporated by him from elsewhere. This is suggested by the opening invocation to the Muses (ii 484–7), and confirmed by good evidence. First, the Catalogue gives not the array of the troops at Troy, which would be suitable for the tenth year of the war, but the mobilization of the ships at Aulis before they sailed to Troy. The text does not mention Aulis at this point, but this is where the ships gather. Each detachment is mentioned with the places from which its men come and the number of its ships. The language is factual, but is saved from severity by the choice of local epithets. The whole passage hangs together, but we can see how Homer has had to adapt it to his tale. For instance, he names both Philoctetes (ii 718), who was left on Lemnos, and Protesilaos (ii 698), who was killed on landing at Troy. Homer adjusts the Catalogue to mention what happened to them, but his adjustments are plainly corrections and additions to a factual list.

The Achaean Catalogue was not devised to suit the *Iliad*, nor the *Iliad* to suit it. There are discrepancies between them. The Boeotians, whose contingent is named first and is the biggest of all, play no part in the poem. The Thessalians, who get considerable attention, do not count elsewhere. More important is the different treatment of certain leading figures, for this difference is not merely of scale or emphasis but of fact. First, Achilles, who is a great chieftain in the poem and whose father Peleus rules as far as Iolcus and Mount Pelion, is confined in the Catalogue to a small part of Thessaly. Secondly, Odysseus, who in the poem seems to be lord of the western isles, gets in the Catalogue a mere dozen ships and yields most of his territory to a certain Meges. Thirdly, Agamemnon, so far from ruling over 'many islands and all Argos', gets no more than what later constituted Corinth, Sicyon and the eastern part of Achaea. The Catalogue is clearly independent of the *Iliad* and earlier than it. When he incorporated it, Homer respected it enough to allow quite serious discrepancies between it and his own picture of the Achaean confederacy.

If the Catalogue is older than the *Iliad*, we must ask how it came into existence, and especially whether it can be derived from a Mycenaean original. As we know from the Pylos tablets, the Mycenaeans had their own dry orders of battle, and it is conceivable that such was drawn up for the Trojan war, though nothing that we have remotely resembles it in scale. A list of this kind has been found at the Ugaritic city of Ras Shamra, and other examples would suit this age of documents and records. But it is impossible to see how such a document could have passed into poetry which lasted long enough for Homer to know it. The Mycenaean script was forgotten long before his time, and we cannot imagine that documents about such a mobilization were taken across the Aegean by colonists who would certainly not have been able to read them. If the Catalogue comes from the far past, it must have come orally in verse, passed from bard to bard and from generation to generation because of its connexion with a resplendent past. This is by no means impossible. In unlettered societies fabulous feats of memory are possible for those who have never learned to rely on books. The kings of Uganda kept official singers who recalled their descent for thirty generations; the Maoris remember in detail the voyages which brought them from Tahiti to New Zealand between *c.* A.D. 825 and *c.* A.D. 1350. We can imagine that at an early date some Greek bard versified a list of the contingents who met at Aulis before going to Troy, and that this was learned and passed on in the usual mnemonic manner. Homer got to know of it and annexed it with the minimum of necessary alterations.

The Catalogue presents a credible picture of late Mycenaean Greece. The Dorians have not arrived, and are therefore not mentioned. Nor are places which were later to become important, such as Megara, Sparta, Corinth, and Argos. Many of the places are known to have been Mycenaean sites, and, what is more relevant, about a quarter of them were not known in historical times and could not be identified. The places are real, and are often presented with epithets which indicate personal knowledge. This presupposes a poetry able to deal with so large a subject and a poet ready to versify it with some elegance. We may with some confidence assume that Homer knew and annexed a poem which was itself more or less Mycenaean and that he himself regarded it as an authority on the heroic past. But what is not so clear is when this poem, in its main lines, was composed, and how trustworthy it is in its present form.

The Catalogue may conceivably have been composed after the mass-movement of the Boeotians from Thessaly into the later Boeotia. Thucydides asserts that this took place some sixty years after the fall of Troy (1.12). This suits Boeotia as the Catalogue presents it, and in that case the whole account of Greece could be in some degree historical. The Dorians are not yet in Crete or in Rhodes, and the diminished realms of Agamemnon and Menelaus reflect the decline in Mycenaean power after the war. But if this is right, and at least it makes sense of the evidence, what we have is a picture of Greece some two generations after the sack of Troy, that is, very soon before the Mycenaean collapse. This is possible, but we do not know how far this picture, ancient though it is, coincides with that of Greece at the actual time of the war. If the composer has given so large a part to the Boeotians, he may have been himself a Boeotian and have exaggerated their power. Changes took place after the Trojan War with the great move of

the Boeotians. If he records this as it was in his own time, may he
not do the same for other regions, notably for the realms of
Achilles and Agamemnon and Odysseus? If he does, then the
Catalogue remains a remarkable document from the Greek past,
but it does not convey trustworthily what Achaean forces went to
Troy. The period after the Trojan War was, according to Thucydides (1.12.2), one of great changes, and these no doubt left their
mark in the Catalogue. The Catalogue looks like an ancient
record but not contemporary with the Trojan War. Somehow
some poet did his best to tell what forces gathered at Aulis, but he
was limited by the circumstances of his time and gave what looks
like an account from two generations later than the Trojan
expedition.

The Catalogue gives figures for the number of ships sent by each
contingent, and these excite distrust. The total of 1,186 seems
impossibly large if they were all to be beached in the Troad. The
words for 'ships' and for the different numbers are Ionic but not
Mycenaean Greek, and look like inventions. It is possible that
some of the entries are dubious because national pride insisted on
adding them after the first composition. Salamis, from which Aias
comes with twelve ships (ii 557–8) gets only two lines and is made
subordinate to Athens. In antiquity this was thought to be an
insertion made by the Athenians in the sixth century (Strabo 394;
Diogenes Laertius 1.48; Quintilian 5.40), and this may be right.
The Catalogue raises many insoluble problems, but in one point
it deserves respect. It embodies a belief that the united Achaeans
formed a huge expedition against Troy. That belief lies behind the
Iliad and cannot be dismissed.

Parallel to the Achaean Catalogue of ships is the Catalogue of
Trojan allies, ii 816–77. It is much shorter and less informative,
and even harder to assess. Once an Achaean Catalogue existed, it
was natural to ask for a Trojan, and since the Trojans did not
have ships, the names of their allies, without numbers, must do.
The Trojan Catalogue is more obviously independent from the
main text than even the Achaean. In the whole poem 216 Trojans
are named, of whom 180 are killed, but the Catalogue gives very

little help. Of its 26 Trojans, 8 do not reappear, and only 5 are of any importance. Clearly whoever composed the Trojan Catalogue was not the poet of the *Iliad*. It is very unlikely to be later than the *Iliad*, for if it were, it would take notice of it; it is an earlier, independent composition, and there is no reason why it should not come from the same time as the Achaean Catalogue, as a necessary pendant to it. At least, the list of peoples named do not fit what we know of Asia Minor after the Ionian colonization which began *c.* 1100, but it would be, so far as we know, suitable for the last days of the Mycenaean world. The author's knowledge is not extensive. He knows much less about the places of Asia Minor than of Greece and its islands, but what he knows does not inspire distrust. It is true that Miletus is given to the Carians (ii 868) though it seems to have been at times a Mycenaean dependency. But when the compiler compiled, it may have reverted to its older state. The Trojan list complements the Achaean, and reports what was believed before the end of the Mycenaean age.

The Homeric poems owe to the Mycenaean age some of their main themes and persons, their sense of a rich and resplendent past, and some elements in their vocabulary. All these were enriched and extended and reshaped to meet new needs of language and habits in the centuries between the Mycenaeans and Homer. The poems are in no real sense Mycenaean; they merely contain some Mycenaean elements. Their vision of a Greek heroic age is highly selective and idealized. In later times gods were sometimes thought to be seen on earth, but not to consort with men as Homer presents them doing. The wealth of the Mycenaean palaces was in fact even greater than Homer thought, if we may compare Homer's number of slaves in a great house with what it was. Odysseus and Alcinous each keep fifty women to work in their houses (7.103; 22.421), but the tablets from Pylos, which come from a single place for a very short period, gives the names of 645 slave-women, together with 370 girls and 210 boys. The Mycenaean age deserved to be honoured as an age of heroes in the scope of its achievements, the scale of its wealth, the splendour of its monuments. No doubt the kings and princes who were later the patrons of heroic song often traced their descent from heroes and were proud to hear of their prowess. This vision of the past gave glory to the present, and found an apogee in the Homeric poems.

The Homeric conception of a heroic age was maintained and enriched through poetry, but the instrument through which this poetry worked was probably itself of Mycenaean origin. The Greek hexameter has no parallel in other Indo-European languages until it is copied by the Romans. In using quantity as the basis of its prosody it resembles Sanskrit, but it uses it for a different measure, and it looks as if it were a Greek invention. An attempt has indeed been made to show that it is pre-Greek and comes from Minoan Crete. It happens that an Egyptian text quotes a spell which it claims to be in the language of the Keftiu (Cretans):

santi kapupi wayya jaja minti lalakali[1]

This *could* sound like a hexameter, but its language is still unknown, and magical spells, especially when quoted by Egyptians, are hardly reliable evidence. On the other hand the hexameter thrives on an essential quality of the Greek language, its balance of short and long syllables and its ability to differentiate decisively between them on the principle that one long is the equivalent of two shorts. This assumption lies behind all Greek metric, and the hexameter is the earliest known example of it at work.

The Greek origin of the hexameter receives some support from the archaic Greek of the tablets in Mycenaean Script B. These are not in verse and have very little relation to its subjects and vocabulary, but they give enough information about early Greek words to show that they could fall without serious difficulty into hexameters. It must of course be an accident that certain phrases on the tablets look as if they were parts of hexameters, but the likeness conceals a significant fact. Because this archaic Greek contained a large number of short syllables, it was possible without much difficulty to operate a metrical system based on the proportion of longs to shorts. A simple test may be taken with proper

[1] H. T. Bossert, quoted by J. Friedrich, *Kleinasiatische Sprachdenkmäle*, 146.

names. Of fifty-eight names for men quoted by the first editors, fifty-two can be fitted without change into hexameters, as can twenty-one place-names of Greek origin in the tablets from Pylos. Nor is this difficult to explain. At this stage of its existence the Greek language still preserved a large number of uncontracted vowels, and, especially in compound words, these betray the metrical potentialities of the language. Its words fall more easily into a dactylic rhythm than do the contracted words of a later age, and though in classical times the iambic may have been close to ordinary speech, this does not seem to be true of the Mycenaean age. Once the hexameter took command as the appropriate measure of heroic song, the poets were free to invent formulae for it and prepare it to meet every emergency of composition. Formulae, once invented and accepted, stayed in use, and that is why Homer has so many connexions with what was already for him a distant past. If the hexameter had been easier to compose, it would have needed fewer and less elaborate formulae and been less conservative in its use of them.

If the hexameter was in use in Mycenaean times, it explains, as nothing else can, why relics of these times appear in the Homeric poems, which must be some five hundred years later. Themes were crystallized into metrical sets of words, and these were memorized and passed on from generation to generation. Many must have perished on the way or been replaced by more up-to-date phrases, but enough survived from early days to keep the succession secure. We cannot say that any single passage or line is genuinely and completely Mycenaean, for the language has changed too much in the interval. But we *can* say that this or that passage is based on a Mycenaean original because this subject or this object existed only in Mycenaean times. In the same way a few words are undoubtedly Mycenaean, and survive partly for their antique air. We need not assume that the Mycenaeans had a heroic poetry on a large scale, but it is likely that they had at least panegyrics and laments in verse which seem to be a common antecedent of heroic poetry. In these the metre and the manner, perhaps even part of the vocabulary, of a coming art were matured. The vital change must have come when bards turned from the present to the past, and the natural time for this to happen was when the Mycenaean world collapsed, and men looked back to it with awe and admiration and wished it to live again through the imagination. The celebration of noble doings called for a majestic metre, and this the hexameter was. Mycenaean poetry need not have borne any close resemblance to its far-off Homeric descendant and may well have been shorter, more clumsy, more brutal, more immediately concerned with the present, but it contained incalculable possibilities of growth, and of these in the succeeding centuries the Ionian bards took advantage.

CHAPTER SIX

The Iliad:
its Shape and Character

THE *Iliad* starts with an invocation to the Muse to sing of what is presumably the main subject of the poem:

Sing, goddess, of the anger of Achilles, son of Peleus, the deadly anger, which brought countless sorrows to the Achaeans, and sent many strong spirits of heroes to Hades, and left their bodies as carrion for dogs and all birds. The plan of Zeus was accomplished. Start from the point when Atreus' son, king of men, and godlike Achilles first quarrelled in conflict. (i 1–7)

A poet is under no obligation to set out his whole theme at the start; he is free to keep surprises in store, and Homer keeps many, but his opening words contain no deception. The *Iliad* certainly deals with the wrath of Achilles and with sorrows and deaths. The only slight oddity is the reference to the plan of Zeus. In antiquity some learned men thought that this was the plan, related in the *Cypria*, by which Zeus decided to reduce the population of the earth by the Trojan War (fr. 1 Allen; scholl. A i.5). The actual words survive, and the last four are identical with Homer's. Yet we may doubt whether Homer means this. He says nothing about it elsewhere, and in so far as he ascribes a divine origin to the Trojan War, it is the resentment which Athene and Hera feel at the judgment of Paris (xxiv 27–30). It is much more likely that the Homeric words refer to the plot of the *Iliad* and specifically to the part played in it by the decision of Zeus, at the request of Thetis, to let the Achaeans be humiliated by defeat while Achilles abstains from battle. This plan holds the different episodes together, and from it arise two main events, the death of Patroclus and the death of Hector.

The plot of the *Iliad* is complex in the sense that the theme of the wrath of Achilles is worked into the larger theme of the fate of Troy. Homer partly prefigures this in his opening words, and his intention may have been to relate the wrath of Achilles to its consequences on a bigger scale than had hitherto been done. The poem has almost a twofold character, telling first of the wrath and its consequences to Achilles himself, his friends and his enemies, and second of the fate of Troy, which is inextricably interwoven with the absence of Achilles from the battlefield or his appearance on it. The poem is not an Achilleid but an Iliad, and this accounts for its scope and scale. The two subjects are closely interrelated, and in the last books united. The richness of the *Iliad* comes from its being concerned with much more than the wrath of Achilles. His fate is central, but the fate of Troy is hardly less so, and in the end, though neither the death of Achilles nor the capture of Troy has a place in the narrative, each is imminent and certain. This combination of two main themes is possible because the short lay has been expanded into the long epic. When the latter was called for, the poet extended his scope from a single theme to a much more complex subject. Once perhaps, the wrath of Achilles was one of many themes attached to the Trojan War; now it is awarded pride of place, and at the same time other themes are brought into relation with it and given a new significance in a new setting.

The wrath of Achilles does much more than give a start to the *Iliad* or account for some of its main actions. It is a commanding theme which passes through different stages until it comes to an end in Book xxiv. It is admirably right for its purpose, for it arises from the heroic view of manhood. When Agamemnon, asserting his powers as commander-in-chief, insists on taking Briseis from Achilles, he insults him in his very being. Achilles has every right to Briseis, but Agamemnon disregards this, and the affront is deadly. Where honour is the rule, a man must pay to others the respect that he demands for himself, and in this

Agamemnon conspicuously fails. Since Agamemnon has denied his dignity, Achilles retaliates by asserting it to the utmost; he decides to absent himself from the battlefield and, by letting the Achaeans be defeated in his absence, show how great his worth is. Honour, when wounded, calls for something to restore it, and this Achilles unerringly and inevitably seeks. The drama of Book i presents the quarrel between him and Agamemnon on a full scale because it is the basis of the whole poem both in the actions which it provokes and in its characterization of Achilles. At the end of it the plan of Achilles to humiliate the Achaeans has won the favour of Zeus and is about to be put into effect.

Books ii to viii tell what happens to the Achaeans in the absence of Achilles. His presence is felt in the background, and at times he is mentioned, but he takes no part in the action, and is not yet interested in it. It is for the other Achaeans to show what they can do without him, but Homer tells much more than this. His poem assumes the dimensions of an Iliad and is centred on the war for Troy. The action is supposed to take place in the tenth year of war (ii 329), but much that is told, such as Helen's account of the Achaean leaders or the duel of Menelaus and Paris, would have been more appropriate for the first year. Once the poet has decided to make his poem an Iliad, he can expand his range without worrying too much about chronology, and the additional material adds breadth and substance. When Achilles abstains from fighting, the results do not appear at once, but the action starts as befits the demands of the larger scheme. Homer plunges into events with a surprising device. Zeus has promised Thetis that the Achaeans will be humiliated, and sets to work by sending to Agamemnon a lying dream which promises that he shall take Troy that very day (ii 23 ff.). This could have dramatic results, since the confidence which it instils into Agamemnon would stress by contrast the degree of his subsequent failure and his depression at it. But this is not what happens. Homer is not content with the dream, but makes Agamemnon decide to test the morale of his army by suggesting that they should all abandon the siege and return home. This is a possible situation in a heroic world, but it destroys the dramatic potentialities of the dream and creates an entirely new situation. The army panics and has to be brought to its senses by Odysseus. The two themes are not very happily joined, and we may surmise that in starting on his large subject Homer was faced by traditional alternatives. In one the false dream preceded disasters; in the other the army panicked and had to be made fit for battle. Either would have made a good start, but perhaps Homer shrank from the exclusive use of the first, because it brought the defeat of the Achaeans too early, and from the second because help from Zeus is needed to enforce his plan. The combination starts the battle, but not in an easy or straightforward way.

This method gives an excuse for introducing the Catalogues of Achaean ships and Trojan allies, which belong to the beginning of the war. Little attempt is made to cover the traces, and it is useful to be told who the antagonists are, even though the lists sometimes give too much and sometimes too little. If the Catalogues were already known and honoured, a poem on the Trojan War might be expected to contain them. Then the action can start, but not yet with a general conflict. An attempt is made to settle the war by a duel between the two men most concerned, Menelaus and Paris. This too would have taken place more suitably at the start of the war, but it fits in well where it is. While preparations for it are made, we are introduced to Helen, who is the cause of the war, and see her as she is seen by Priam and the old men of Troy. They know well what the armies are fighting for, and they comment:

'It is no matter for indignation that Trojans and well-greaved Achaeans should suffer sorrows for a long time for such a woman; she is terribly like the immortal goddesses to look upon.' (3.156–8)

Helen then identifies some of the Achaean leaders to Priam, and this helps us to know them. The duel is inconclusive, because Aphrodite snatches Paris away in a cloud, and then at last the battle proper begins.

Books v to viii are occupied with fighting, and their dominant feature is that at first the Achaeans, without Achilles, do quite well. The young Diomedes, after being unjustly chidden by Agamemnon, pursues a victorious career and does not shrink from attacking gods. He has the glamour and the gallantry of youth, and for a time takes the place of Achilles. Other Achaeans emulate him, not without success, but the main pattern is set by the entry into battle of the Trojan Hector, who soon makes his force felt, and drives back the Achaeans until at the end of Book viii the Trojans are encamped on the plain between the Achaean camp and the walls of Troy. So far the plan of Achilles has succeeded, not overwhelmingly, but still dangerously for his fellow warriors. The theme is still that of an Iliad, and Troy receives ample attention. Its life is richer and more varied than that of the Achaean camp, and we get a first glimpse of it when Priam speaks to Helen on the wall. Later, two other scenes add striking touches of humanity. When Paris is spirited away from the battlefield, Aphrodite tells Helen to go to him. Helen reproaches the goddess with her cruelty and speaks bitterly of her own humiliating state, but Aphrodite is obdurate and Helen yields (iii 383 ff.). Later, when Hector goes into Troy, he meets his wife and little child, and their interchange with its noble pathos and complete truth is far removed from the furies of the battlefield, and a fine contrast and background to them (vi 394 ff.). Against the almost exclusively masculine society of the Achaeans, with its fierce pride and emulous pursuit of honour, Homer sets these brief interludes in Troy with its old men and young wives, its insecurity and its sense of doom.

Book ix moves back to the wrath of Achilles. The book treats him with inspired attention, with a full grasp of what his decision means to him as well as to others, and it is hard to imagine the *Iliad* without this full delineation of a great hero at a time of fierce crisis. The book begins with the Achaean leaders in a turmoil of anxiety at the success of the Trojan onslaught. At Nestor's suggestion Agamemnon says that he is willing to make amends, since he acted in infatuation of mind (ix 119) and is now ready to make handsome payment to Achilles for his injured honour. This is correct procedure, and the other leaders approve. They seem to think that Achilles will accept, and Odysseus and Aias, accompanied by old Phoenix, go to his tent. Achilles gives them a courteous welcome, listens to what they have to say, and then states his own case. Though the envoys treat this as a refusal, they have to some degree touched him; for Homer marks three stages in his reaction to them. First, he says that he proposes to sail home on the morrow (ix 357), and he supports his decision with the passionate argument that the effort of war is not worth while, for a man has only one life and no price can buy it once it has gone (ix 406–9). Then, after listening to the long speech of Phoenix on the dangers of anger, he makes a correction, and says that with the dawn he will decide whether to go home or to stay where he is (ix 618–19). Finally, after some sturdy words from Aias, he takes another step forward and says that he will think of fighting when Hector breaks through to the ships and the tents of the Myrmidons (ix 650–5). Achilles has in fact made a considerable concession. It is not all that the Achaeans want, but in the course of making it, he has fought a notable struggle with himself, and there is a faint ray of hope. That no doubt is why after a gloomy reception of his message, which certainly promises no immediate help, the Achaeans prepare to resume battle in their own strength.

Book x is an interlude, a chapter of night-operations before the main battle starts again. It differs in many ways, notably in a certain brutality of tone, from much of the *Iliad*, and it has reasonably been regarded as a later addition. In antiquity there were those who thought it an early work of Homer himself, and even if it is not his, it is not necessarily later. It contains remarkable archaic material in the account of a helmet made of boars' teeth (x 261–5), but, whatever its origin, it provides an interlude between the tensions and frustrations of Book ix and the resumption of battle in Book xi. The plot now shifts back from Achilles to the general theme of war, but inside this there are marked movements. In turn Achaean leaders go out and fight. They begin well but are in turn wounded and forced to retire. The dominating figure is Hector who inspires the Trojans to attack the Achaean camp. The crisis comes when they break through the protecting

26–30. ABOVE: *Phoenix with Briseis, cause of the quarrel between Achilles and Agamemnon (see p. 98).* OVERLEAF, TOP LEFT: *Hector bids a tender farewell to his wife Andromache (see p. 36).* LOWER LEFT: *Achilles and Patroclus.* TOP RIGHT: *the funeral games held in honour of Patroclus after Hector's death* LOWER RIGHT: *Hector and Achilles fighting; Hector is bleeding.*

31, 32. *A skyphos of* c. 480 B.C. *by the Brygos painter. The bearded figure on the lower picture represents Priam, begging Achilles for the body of his son Hector, lying beneath the couch (see pp. 40, 176)*

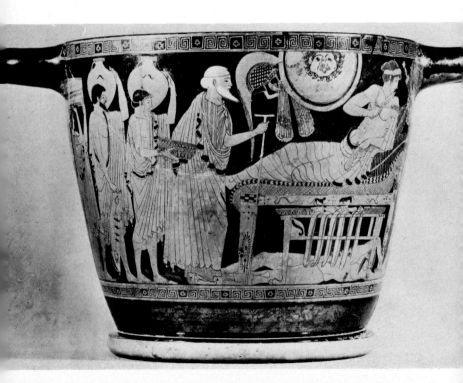

wall and bring fire to the beached ships. At this point the prayer of
Achilles is really answered, and we might expect him to return to
battle. But Homer moves with more subtlety and prepares the way
to a new climax.

The new movement is anticipated by skilful preparation. So far
we have heard very little of Patroclus, the friend of Achilles, who
is older than he is (xi 787), shares everything with him and like
him has abstained from battle. He now begins to count, but not at
a single stroke. Homer insinuates him into the narrative. When
Achilles, who has been watching the Achaean retreat, sees a
wounded man brought to Nestor's tent, he wishes to know who it
is and sends Patroclus to find out (xi 608 ff.). Patroclus stays with
Nestor, learns how grave the situation is, and promises that he will
tell Achilles (xi 839). A little later, when the danger is greatest,
Zeus tells Hera that Achilles will send Patroclus to battle, where
he will be killed (xv 64–7). At this point Patroclus is not with
Achilles but with the wounded Eurypylus with whom he shares
the general despondency in face of defeat (xv 390 ff.). In this
company he knows what a soldier's task is and decides that he
must go to Achilles and urge him to fight (xv 402).

Once he is back with Achilles Patroclus does not press him to
fight, which might be useless, but instead asks Achilles to lend
him his armour that he may deceive and frighten the Trojans and
provide some respite in the battle (xvi 38 ff.). The change of
purpose is not explained, but we surmise that Patroclus prefers to
take on himself the main responsibility, perhaps in the hope that
it may inspire Achilles to join him. In any case Patroclus plays the
main part. Achilles yields, and the action proceeds with solemnity
as he makes a libation to Zeus and prays that Patroclus may drive
off the enemy and return home safely. The new stage is marked by
a detailed marshalling of the Myrmidons, and then Patroclus starts
his career of glory. The Trojans are soon in full retreat and
Patroclus thrice scales the wall of Troy only to be thrust down on
each occasion by Apollo (xvi 702–3). The prayer of Achilles has
been answered. The success of his policy is justified by Patroclus,
and his honour is to this extent restored.

Patroclus triumphs at first, and then is killed, and the armour of Achilles is in the possession of Hector. Achilles seems to have had no fear that the worst would happen, but Zeus, who cannot save his son Sarpedon from Patroclus, is not prepared to save Patroclus from Hector. So far as success in battle is concerned, Achilles' prayer is answered, but at a terrible price. The strength of his feeling for Patroclus is to be gauged not from the mildly playful way in which he teases him about his anxiety (xvi 7 ff.), but from his uncontrolled grief at hearing of his death (xviii 22 ff.). His anger against Agamemnon is now finished, and he will soon go through the formalities of reconciliation, but the wrath has changed its direction and grown in fierceness. It is now turned against Hector and will be satisfied only by his death (xviii 90–3). With this change the *Iliad* enters on its last long phase, in which the wrath of Achilles and the fate of Troy are brought into a single strand. Achilles on the battlefield makes all the other Achaeans of no account, and his pursuit of other enemies is preliminary to his pursuit of Hector.

Achilles' actions up to the killing of Hector have a relentless, increasing momentum equalled by no other hero. He is driven by an uncurbed passion in his merciless treatment of Lycaon (xxi 34 ff.), his fight with the river-god Scamander (xxi 136 ff.), his defiance of Apollo (xxii 15 ff.) and his final fight with Hector. He carries all before him, as his irresistible strength is kept in action by his concentrated and consuming anger. It is true that Hector is abandoned and betrayed by the gods, but he is clearly marked for destruction, and the final encounter is brief and deadly. Achilles treats the dying Hector with scorn and brushes aside his prophecies of doom (xxii 365–6). He has killed his enemy and is in possession of his body, and his exultation finds voice in his boast to his followers:

'We have won great glory; we have killed godlike Hector, to whom the Trojans offered prayers in the city as to a god.' (xxii 393–4)

With this an apparent end is reached. Achilles has wreaked his vengeance on Hector; the death of Hector is a portent of the fall of Troy. When the Trojans see his body dragged behind the chariot of Achilles, Priam knows what it means:

To him it was most like as if all beetling Troy were consumed with fire from the summit. (xxii 410–11)

The two main themes come together in this tragic consummation, but there is still something to be said.

Though the death of Hector means the end of Troy, that end lies beyond the scope of the *Iliad*; it is a theme too vast to fit into the present scheme. So also, just as Hector's death is payment for the death of Patroclus, so Achilles will in turn pay when Paris and Apollo kill him (xxii 358–60). But this too lies outside the *Iliad*. Homer reaches a crisis with the death of Hector, but is not content to stop there. The wrath, which is the mainspring of the poem, is not fully healed, nor will it be by the mere act of vengeance. Blood thrives on blood, and we expect more. Moreover, since Achilles himself is soon to die, it is appropriate that he should first recover his balance. Homer has this in mind, for though he finishes before the death of Achilles, his last two books are given to the latest stages of the wrath and its final healing.

As yet it is not enough for Achilles to have killed Hector, to have let his Myrmidons pierce the body with their spears, to drag it round the walls of Troy. He stills plans outrages against it and thinks of throwing it to the dogs (xxiii 21), while it is part of his fury that he sacrifices twelve young Trojan prisoners at the pyre of Patroclus (xxiii 22–3; 175–6), and the poet expressly says that he 'plotted shameless doings' (xxii 395; xxiii 24). During the funeral and the funeral-games Achilles controls himself, but when these are over, we wonder what will happen to Hector's body and fear something hideous. But the gods keep it from corruption, and then Homer springs his magnificent surprise. The gods arrange for Priam to go by night to the tent of Achilles and ransom the body. At last the fury which has long dominated Achilles passes away, not into any mere absence of emotion but into noble compassion for old Priam. There is a hint that the fury is not quite dead when Achilles warns Priam not to provoke him (xxiv 568–70), but it lasts for only a moment. The essence and the splendour of Book xxiv are that the fury which has consumed Achilles and caused so many disasters comes to an end in an act of mercy. Though he has lost his only friend, and though his own death is near, neither of these counts with him. What matters is that at the end of the poem Achilles regains the heroic balance of temper which was so gravely shaken at the outset.

In reaching this climax the *Iliad* follows a simple but emphatic plan. Book i sets the scene for all that is to follow and presents the main Achaean characters. Book ii–ix set out the preliminaries of battle, then the battle itself, the Achaean reverses, and the attempt in Book ix to persuade Achilles to come back to war. This is a failure, and the first main line of action closes in gloom. Books x–xx give the second main movement. Book x is an interlude but at least takes the story back to fighting. This increases in scale and ferocity and in losses to the Achaeans. Achilles lets Patroclus go to battle and death, with the result that in xx Achilles is reconciled with Agamemnon. Books xxi–xxiv tell how Achilles reverses the fortune of war, kills Hector, conducts the funeral of Patroclus and releases Hector's body to Priam. This masterly development is marked by a certain formality of design. In Book i the wrath of Achilles begins and Thetis goes to Zeus; in Book xxiv the wrath is healed after Zeus has sent Thetis to Achilles. The outbreak of wrath is matched by its healing. There is also a balance between Books ii and xxiii. Book ii starts with a dream and leads to the outbreak of war and both armies on the march; Book xxiii begins with another dream, but it leads to the appeasement of Achilles and the friendly contests of the Achaean leaders. We may even see a balance between the indecisive fight between Menelaus and Paris in Book iii and the decisive fight between Achilles and Hector in xxii. The poet, who enjoyed diversions and variety, had in mind a master plan, and worked skilfully within it.

Such seems to be the main plan of the *Iliad*, and the outward form fits the dramatic development. A dominating pattern is imposed on what might have been vaguely connected episodes. The twofold scheme is equally successful in each of its parts.

While the personal doom of Achilles attains a noble personal grandeur, the fortunes of Troy and its people give variety and authenticity to the heroic narrative. Inevitably the poem devotes much time to fighting, as heroic poetry always does, and the *Iliad* is perhaps less extravagant than much other poetry on like themes. It is inevitable that there should be many combats and woundings and deaths, for these are the stuff of such poetry, but their handling may vary enormously and make different claims on us. First, the single combat is normal and familiar to societies which cultivate heroic poetry. Even when it becomes less common, it thrives as a theme for song, and blows dealt and taken in such combats are appreciated by listeners who fancy themselves as connoisseurs. Even in our own ignorance of such matters we can see that Homer does very well. His single combats take many forms; wounds, usually fatal, have an ingenious variety; the antics of the dying have a gruesome verisimilitude. Moreover, though the single combat is normal, at times mass movements take its place, as when the Trojans break the Achaean wall (xii 430 ff.) or Patroclus leads the Myrmidons to battle (xvi 257 ff.). In both kinds of conflict a clear vision sees what happens and marks its course and consequences. Remote though much of the action is from our own experience, we can share some of its excitement and appreciate that a single combat is regarded as the ultimate test of a man's worth, with all the thrills of an athletic contest but with the artistic advantage of a fatally final result.

Homer saw that at times the carnage called for relief, and one method was to bring it into proximity with scenes of a more peaceful character. So when Helen talks to Priam on the wall (iii 121 ff.), the killing has not in fact begun, and it makes its contrast when it comes after this affectionate and touching colloquy. The scene between Hector and Andromache (vi 369 ff.) breaks a long line of battle-scenes and throws a new, human light on war. When Briseis comes back to Achilles, she finds the dead body of Patroclus in the tent, and laments for him, as do the other women with her, 'in name for Patroclus, but each at heart for her own sorrows' (xix 302). Though Thetis is a goddess, she has a deep love for her

son, and his sorrows are hers. When she first comes to him out of
the sea and hears of his humiliation by Agamemnon, she refers to
his doom of a short life and laments that even in this he is con-
demned to misery (i 414–18). She shares his grief at the death of
Patroclus as if it were also her tragedy and laments in words of
which Plato disapproved (*Republic* iii 388c), 'Alas, for my misery,
who am the unhappy mother of the noblest of men' (xviii 54). Yet
her love for her son is not blind, and when the gods wish him to
end his wrath and give back Hector's body, she tells him to do so,
and he obeys (xxiv 128 ff.).

These touches from family and home, even if they are as
unusual as those of Achilles, stress the uncertainty and insecurity
of heroic life. Among his own comrades, on his own field of battle,
the hero is sure of himself and his prowess, but in his scheme of
things nothing is certain, and this makes his affections his most
vulnerable place. Achilles is hideously hurt through the death of
Patroclus (xviii 98 ff.); Hector knows that, if he himself is killed,
his wife will be sold into slavery (vi 454 ff.), and she herself
foresees the despised lot that will fall to her little son (xxii 490 ff.).
Hector fights for his family as he fights for his city, but they are
not all that he fights for. He is not so complete or so redoubtable a
hero as Achilles, but he is the second foremost warrior on the
battlefield, and his prowess is inspired by a similar lust for honour
in accomplishing all that he possibly can.

If domestic scenes give one additional dimension, the gods give
another. We may perhaps assume that they always had some part
in poetry of this kind, as they had in the epics of the Near and
Middle East. In *Gilgamesh* they intervene in the actions of men
and shape their destinies, and though men are defeated, it is only
after they have put up a very stubborn fight. In the *Iliad* the gods
are less dominating, but they are not insignificant. Though they
may be said to have started the war because of the judgment of
Paris, this is not revealed until near the end (xxiv 25–30), and
though the alignment of gods and goddesses between the two
opposing armies is to be explained partly by this and partly by a
low trick played on Poseidon by the Trojan king Laomedon

(xxi 441 ff.), we do not attach much significance to it. The gods enrich the tale because at times they interfere in the action and display their own preferences. But their powers are limited. Zeus indeed gives in to Thetis and starts the rout of the Achaeans, but when his son Sarpedon is confronted by Patroclus, Zeus is over-ruled in any attempt to save him (xvi 431 ff.), just as any compassion that he may feel for Hector is at once countered by Athene (xxii 177 ff.), and his doom is settled by the divine scales (xxii 209–12). Though the gods have some say in what happens, their word is not always final.

The gods sometimes take part in the battle, and this looks like an ancient feature of heroic song. But Homer sets limits to it. On the whole men do not attack gods. One exception is Diomedes, who attacks Aphrodite, knowing that she is not a formidable warrior (v 330 ff.), and wounds her, proving himself right when she retires weeping. He also prepares to attack Apollo (v 434), but the god warns him off, and he desists. This does not prevent him from attacking and wounding Ares, whose roar is like that of nine or ten thousand men (v 860) and may be explained by his fury at the injury to his honour. Diomedes is young, and has been carried away, but he does not repeat his attacks on the gods and soon enough disclaims anything of the kind (vi 129). The only other case is when Achilles fights the river-god Scamander. He is no Olympian, but he is a formidable opponent, and it takes a warrior of Achilles' stature to defy him. The fight soon involves other, more powerful gods, and develops into a new action. In general Homeric heroes do not fight with the gods any more than they oppose their will in other matters. In this Homer differs from the poet of *Gilgamesh*, who sets his two heroes in almost direct conflict with the gods and adds greatly to their heroism by it.

On the other hand the gods interfere in human warfare. In general they support their friends and attack their enemies, and pay no attention to what men regard as the decencies of war. When Paris is on the point of being killed by Menelaus in a duel, Aphrodite releases him and transports him safe to his own chamber in Troy (iii 380–3). So too Aeneas is rescued from battle by his mother Aphrodite (v 311 ff.) and later by Poseidon from Achilles (xx 321 ff.). Similarly the gods attack as well as protect. When Patroclus scales the wall of Troy, Apollo thrusts him down (xvi 702–3), finally wounds him in the back and makes him drop his helmet (xvi 790–8). Even Hector, who defends Troy for which Apollo fights, is treated harshly by gods on both sides. Athene is against him, and it is she who stops Zeus from putting off his death (xxii 178–81). She makes victory easier for Achilles by taking the form of Deiphobus, as if to help Hector, and then vanishing when help is needed (xxii 295). Once the scales have told against Hector, Apollo deserts him (xxii 213) and leaves him to his death. There are limits to the loyalty of the gods, and men suffer from them. Such a desertion illustrates the fragility of the human state, and though Hector can never really hope that he will kill Achilles, he is in fact allowed very little chance of doing so.

The interference of the gods in human affairs is not confined to limited issues like these. They may start large movements going, as Apollo starts the quarrel of Agamemnon and Achilles (i 8–9), or Iris, at the bidding of Zeus, tells Hector that the Achaeans are preparing for war (ii 786), or Athene persuades Pandarus to break the truce (iv 69 ff.), but having persuaded him diverts his arrow, so that Menelaus is not seriously wounded (iv 130). On the battlefield the gods interfere constantly by directing or deflecting weapons and in their different ways Hera, Athene and Poseidon all play a determining part, while Zeus lays down general lines of behaviour and expects them to be observed. This divine participation is real and natural; both Homer and his audience must have believed that in war there is a large element beyond human control in the charge of the gods. What a less trustful people would assign to luck, the early Greeks assigned to the gods, but this does not make the human actors mere automata in a divine game. They pursue their own aims and deal their own blows; the gods may help or obstruct them, but success or failure remains their own. The gods have the last word, but in the interval men do their utmost and win glory for it. Though Homer talks often enough about fate, he does not see men as victims of a predestined doom. Even the gods are limited by fate, which sets limits to all kinds of actions.

Though the gods must be treated seriously in their behaviour to men, they need not in their behaviour to one another. When they fight, as they do in Book xx, their wounds do not matter, since they have in their veins not blood but a fluid called *ikhor* (v 340). These scenes are not to be taken very solemnly; they are meant to entertain. The laughter is not of scepticism but of belief which is so sure of itself that it is not afraid of ridiculing what it believes. This spirit pervades the badinage and mockery which are normal on Olympus, but it comes out with more splendour in the brilliant episode in which Zeus is beguiled into love and sleep by Hera that the gods may, unperceived by him, take part in the battle. She enhances all her charms and lures him to sleep with her as when they first loved, 'unseen by their dear parents' (xiv 296). As they lie together on Mount Gargarus, flowers—'dewy lotus, and crocus, and soft, crowded hyacinth' (xiv 348–9)—spring up around them, and they are wrapped in a golden cloud. Zeus is handsomely gulled, and there is more than a touch of comedy when he tells Hera that he desires her more than any of his other lovers whom he enumerates (xiv 315–28). It is delightfully light-hearted, graceful and charming, and Zeus keeps his dignity in the force of his desire. The episode breaks the monotony of battle and takes us into a totally different world of fancy. It may be derived from some single, separate lay, rather like that of Demodocus in the *Odyssey* in which the exposure of the love of Ares and Aphrodite awakes the unquenchable laughter of the gods (8.266–366). Such lays may have had a long and popular past, and Homer seized a good chance to introduce his Deception of Zeus where he did. It is beautifully built and balanced and provides pure enjoyment. Such affairs are not part of human life but provide a contrast with it.

Because the gods cannot die, because even their wounds are trivial, they cannot be heroic or win the special glory of heroism. This men can and do, and it is their greatest claim, their special grandeur, their one superiority to the gods. In the pursuit of glory prudence is a secondary consideration which may have to be brushed aside. In the *Iliad*, Polydamas is renowned for his counsel (xviii 249), but when he advises Hector to give up the attack on the Achaean wall (xii 210) or to retire into the city (xviii 254), his advice is rejected, and Hector stands out more clearly as a hero for rejecting it. The pursuit of prowess neglects consideration of risk, and even seeks it for its own sake or as a proof of courage. Courage thrives on danger, and the hero does not care if it means his own death. So when Sarpedon stirs Glaucus to action, he says:

'But now, since on all sides countless dooms of death stand near, which no man can avoid or escape, let us go and win glory either for our enemy or for ourselves.' (xii 326–8)

With Achilles the sense of coming doom is almost an obsession. Despite his own, short attempt to get away from it (ix 356 ff.) he is driven through battle by his sense that he must do what he can in the short time at his disposal. It is this which gives so terrible a force to his cruel words to Lycaon:

'But, friend, you too must die. Why do you lament in this way? Patroclus died, who was a much better man than you. Do you not see what a man I am, beautiful and big? I am the son of a noble father, and a goddess was the mother who bore me, but over me also stand death and overmastering doom. There will be a morning, or a dusk, or a midday, when someone will take my life from me in war, striking me with a spear or with an arrow from the bowstring.' (xxi 106–13)

This is the destiny of every hero, who faces the dangers of battle and knows that before long he will be their victim. The Homeric hero expects no reward beyond honour and glory, and he knows that when he dies, these are all that will survive.

In presenting heroes in action Homer implies conceptions of worth and conduct, and we must ask how far these were determined by his belief that he was telling about an age which was different from his own and in some ways superior to it. This was partly a matter of physical prowess, but it was also a matter of style and other kinds of superiority. No doubt tradition preserved something, believing it to be proper for the grand past, but Homer made use of it and treated it consistently, as if he understood what it meant and what it demanded from him. We accept without question a certain nobility of tone in the *Iliad*, and it lies largely in heroes treating their friends with courtesy and consideration and their enemies with merciless fury. There are exceptions but they prove the rule. In their separate ways Thersites and Dolon fall below the heroic norm, but the former is chastised for it (ii 265 ff.), and the latter is contemptuously killed (x 455–7). Otherwise the persons of the *Iliad*, men and women, Achaeans and Trojans, move with style and with truth to themselves. Their frequent speeches reveal their natures and their reactions to events, their comments on what happens, and a simple underlying philosophy. They react immediately to emotions, notably to anger, which is prominent equally between foes and friends and reflects that self-respect which rejects anything unworthy of heroic honour. They face their problems bravely and squarely and say exactly what they mean about them. There is no irony, no deceit, no concealment. The great spate of spoken words is kept going by powerful emotions. Achilles and Agamemnon are equally violent in their quarrel; Hector and Andromache are equally free of false hopes for the future.

This brave candour reflects the self-regard which inspires heroic behaviour. A man or a woman knows what is expected of him, and to this he conforms. If he falls below it, as Paris is told by Hector that he does (iii 39 ff.; xiii 769), he accepts the reproof and tries to make amends. There is no doubt of what is expected of a hero. This is the main principle of Homeric manhood, and it is equally active in <u>old Priam</u> when he sets out into the night to ransom his son's body and in young Patroclus, who is ashamed that the Achaeans suffer defeat when Achilles abstains from battle. All men are judged by the same standard; Achaeans and Trojans are equal before it. If Achilles is superior to Hector, it is by physical endowment; so far as heroism is concerned there is nothing to choose between them. Yet in another way Achilles differs not only from Hector but from other heroes on both sides. Apart from Patroclus, he has no friends, and though he is on good terms with Odysseus and Aias, he is not intimate. He is the kind of hero who lives largely for himself and his own honour, as Sigurth does in Germanic legend. He is present at Troy presumably because it allows him to show his prowess, and he certainly is not committed to fighting for the recovery of Helen, but asks: 'Do the sons of Atreus, alone among mortal men, love their wives?' (ix 340). Yet even with this difference Achilles is like other heroes; but being more heroic and more conscious of his doom, he does even better what they all do well.

The heroic style excludes certain activities which are unworthy of a full man. He must not fight unfairly in battle, and even an archer, such as Pandarus or Paris, is not regarded as a warrior in the full sense (xi 385). This may have some foundation in history. The original Achaeans may not have used bows and arrows any more than their successors, the Philistines, did against Rameses III, when they paid heavily for it. In other aspects of heroic refusal and rejection we may detect the poet's own preferences in his picture of the heroic world. Outside Homer, legend, as it eventually found its way into tragedy but must have first been known through oral song, abounds in horrors, in incest, parricide, matricide, mutilation, torture. Some of them are just mentioned by Homer, and for a moment we think that Achilles will mutilate the dead Hector. But on the whole such horrors are remarkably absent both from the *Iliad* and also from the *Odyssey*, where we are not actually told that Orestes kills his mother. This sensitivity is the poet's own reaction to heroic stories. He has his own firm, imaginative conception of a heroic age, and obeys it.

Though Homer must have been indebted to tradition for episodes and tales which stressed the energy and endurance of heroes, he must also have drawn on his own observation to give substance to his story. Though he need not have portrayed people realistically, his strong hold on the living scene must come from more than the formulaic words of earlier poets, and reflect his own concern. The *Iliad* brings together the heroic past and the known present, and though the second is kept in full control and seldom allowed to reveal itself fully except in the similes and on the shield of Achilles, yet it gives depth and strength to the heroic action. We need not think that Homer's own world was like that of this Achilles—remote, magnificent, almost more than human. His Achilles is a great imaginative creation, the embodiment of grand ideals which men had matured through the centuries and for which they found the final image in this man of men and hero of heroes. Achilles would be impossible if there had not existed a belief in a heroic age when men were stronger and braver than now.

Against him, in full contrast, stands Hector. He provides a balance to Achilles and wins victories for the Trojans when Achilles is away from the battlefield. The early songs about Achilles must have provided him with a suitably formidable antagonist, and Homer's Hector is perhaps the latest of a succession devised for this dramatic need. The strength of the contrast is between the natural, sympathetic humanity of Hector and the remote, terrifying magnificence of Achilles. We cannot imagine that Hector would abstain from battle on a point of injured honour, or that he would shape his thoughts about life and death into the powerful form which Achilles gives to his. Hector fits into his setting; Achilles is above and beyond his, and comes near to destroying it. It is easy, and not necessarily wrong, to say that Achilles embodies the heroic age as seen in retrospect, while Hector embodies the organized social life of the Greek city as it has formed and found itself in the eighth century. Yet this is not everything. Homer may well have conceived the two personalities as representing different kinds of manhood, each of which was quite convincing. Of Achilles he no doubt knew something from tradition, but with Hector this is not so clear. His name is Greek and means 'holder', which suits the protector and guardian of Troy (vi 403). The existence of a king Hector of Chios about 800 may suggest that the name was already known from poetical tradition (Ion of Chios, 278 F 1), but of course the name may have come from an ancient family tradition. What counts is the place of Hector in the *Iliad*, and here the creative master shows his hand in combining Hector's formidable prowess in battle with his human tenderness and affection. The many strands in the *Iliad*, some very ancient, some less so, are brought together in a grand design, in which the wrath of Achilles and the fate of Troy are closely interwoven, and the manner of interweaving marks different levels in the story, from the dark misgivings of Achilles to the touching tenderness of Hector and Andromache. We could remove this or that part of the *Iliad*, and it would still have a plot and shape, but any substantial removal would damage the pattern and the balance of the whole. Even Book x, most suspected of books, gives a breathing space in the narrative when, after the refusal of Achilles, the Achaeans must brace themselves to a tremendous effort without him.

It is natural to speak of the *Iliad* as in some sense a tragic poem. This is applied most easily to Achilles, who through his decision to humiliate Agamemnon, loses Patroclus. Yet this kind of mistake is common to heroic poetry, and is not exclusively or necessarily tragic. The hero makes his decision on grounds of honour, and pays heavily for it. We see the same process at work in the *Song of Roland* and in *Maldon*, and it is central to the heroic outlook. A disastrous decision of this kind is different from the decisions which bring catastrophe in tragedy proper. Here we are concerned with something that cannot be shirked without loss of honour, but the mistakes of real tragedy are usually due to some fault of character or intelligence, to some excess or defect of personality which blinds the victim to reality and leads him to doom. The tragic hero might act otherwise than as he does; the heroic hero cannot. This is the clue to Achilles and also to Hector, perhaps even to Troy. The heroic world is moved by this principle, and gets from it its grandeur and its austerity. Glory may be some kind of reward; the fulfilment of the heroic life lies in doing to the utmost what honour demands.

CHAPTER SEVEN

The Odyssey:
its Shape and Character

THE *Odyssey*, like the *Iliad*, begins with an invocation to the Muse:

Tell, Muse, of the man of many devices, who wandered far indeed, when he had sacked the holy citadel of Troy. He saw the cities of many men and knew their minds, and many were the sorrows which he suffered in his spirit on the sea, when he tried to win his own life and the return of his companions. But not even so, for all his desire, did he save his companions; for they were destroyed by their own insolence, when they ate the cattle of the Sun Hyperion; and he robbed them of the day of their return. From what point you will, goddess, daughter of Zeus, speak to us also. (1.1–10)

This presents several surprises. Unlike Achilles at the start of the *Iliad*, the hero of the *Odyssey* is not named but called 'the man of many devices', which indicates that his story is familiar, and this is confirmed by the last words when the muse is asked to 'speak to us also'. But the familiar story is outlined in a peculiar way. The fantastic adventures of Odysseus are inadequately, almost deceptively, suggested in the reference to cities and minds; almost the only city seen by him is the capital of Phaeacia, and minds are not what he marks in the Cyclops and other monsters. Next, the emphasis on his struggle to save his own life is fair enough and anticipates some of his bravest efforts, but he hardly does so much to secure the return of his comrades. He looks after them, but he takes risks with their lives, and more than once he is the cause of their loss. Finally, not a word is said about the Suitors and the vengeance on them. They occupy more than half the poem and provide its central theme. The opening lines of the *Odyssey* are much less apt and less relevant than those of the *Iliad*.

Odysseus must have been the subject of many different stories, some of which survive outside the *Odyssey*, and even of the more constant stories there were variations, as we can see from the Homeric text. When Homer announces his theme at the start, he assumes that much will be known about Odysseus, and the special surprises which he has in store are not of the kind to be publicised now. It is enough that he should refer vaguely to the wanderings and the sufferings of Odysseus and that he should hint at his ultimate return home. It is more striking that he makes such a point of the comrades and their untoward doom, and this is more than a passing whim. One of the chief features of the *Odyssey* is that at the crisis of his fortunes Odysseus has to act alone. Calypso can do little to help him, and on Ithaca he has to find what support he can, first from Eumaeus and then from Tele-machus. Therefore his comrades must be disposed of, and their eating of the cattle of the sun meets a real need in the story. Because of this Odysseus' last ship is wrecked, and he himself is cast up on Calypso's island. Homer does not actually give false clues, but his clues are a little delusive. His aim is to keep his audience guessing about how he will treat a familiar mass of stories, which none the less have to be selected and remodelled to suit his own taste.

The material of the *Odyssey* differs greatly from that of the *Iliad* and gives it a different character. While the *Iliad* tells of the 'glorious doings of men' and is heroic in the sense that heroes struggle against other heroes, the *Odyssey* uses a less specific and less exalted material. Its stories are ultimately fairy-tales or folk-tales, and are unheroic in the sense that the unquestionable hero Odysseus is faced not by his equals but by his inferiors or by monsters. In its own compass it displays two kinds of narrative. Books 1–4 and 13–24 tell the age-old tale of the Wanderer's Return and his vengeance on the Suitors who devour his substance and try to marry his wife. In this there is not much fantasy or marvel. Instead we find what 'Longinus' calls 'a comedy of manners' (*On the Sublime* 9.15). By this he means that it is concerned with the behaviour of human beings at a familiar and not very exalted level, as he himself knew it in the comedies of Menander. So far as it goes, this is fair enough, as is also his judgment on Books v–xii, in which he speaks of 'a fancy roving in the fabulous and incredible' (ibid. 9.13). The two parts differ greatly in matter, scale, temper and outlook. The second consists of stories so ancient that they seem to have been polished and perfected by constant telling, while the first class, which deals with stories hardly less ancient but of a different kind, has a less confident and less accomplished, even more experimental and more tentative, air.

The *Odyssey* serves in some sense as a sequel to the *Iliad*. No doubt there were many such sequels, especially in the creative heyday of oral song. The tale of Troy had many consequences, and among these were the adventures of Odysseus. In time he became the chief of the surviving heroes, and his return the most famous of many. Once a figure becomes known for certain qualities, appropriate adventures, with which he may originally have had no connexion, are attached to him and marked with his personal imprint. Odysseus seems from the start to have been 'wily' and 'much-enduring', and stories which turned on wiliness or endurance were annexed to him. The relation of the *Odyssey* to the *Iliad* is obvious throughout. The past in retrospect is seen to have been disastrous, the story of 'evil Ilium not to be named' (19.260,597; 23.19), words which do not occur in the *Iliad* and suggest a shift of attitude towards the Trojan War. At the start of the *Odyssey*, when the gods discuss the fate of Odysseus as he languishes on Calypso's island, they turn at once to the fate of his old comrade, Agamemnon, who has been murdered by his wife and her lover (1.35 ff.), and this broaches the topic of what happens to the heroes of Troy. The audience knows all about the Trojan War and can take any reference to it. So now it lies in the background as they hear about Odysseus and Ithaca.

In the *Odyssey* certain characters appear who have played a substantial part in the *Iliad* but need not necessarily play any part in the return of Odysseus. When Telemachus sails off to find news of his father, he visits first Nestor at Pylos and then Menelaus and Helen at Sparta. Nestor is just the same as in the *Iliad*, garrulous, generous, helpful, even wise. Actually he contributes very little to Telemachus' knowledge of his father, and Homer shows a flicker of playful malice when Telemachus, eager to embark on his ship at Pylos and get home, decides to do so without seeing Nestor, since this would waste a lot of time (15.199–201), and sends the young Peisistratus to fix things with him. Menelaus is a less marked personality than Nestor, but he shows the kingly qualities which we expect from him, and especially loyalty to the son of his old friend Odysseus. More striking is Helen, who makes only a few appearances in the *Iliad* but in all of them reveals the pathos of her doom and her desire to escape from it. Her capacity for affection is clear from what she says to Priam (iii 172), to Hector in his lifetime (vi 344 ff.) and about him after his death (xxiv 762 ff.). The whole adventure with Paris has been a sorrow and a disaster for her, but she has not been able to avoid it (iii 399 ff.). Now she is back with Menelaus at Sparta, happy and at peace. She recalls without distress episodes from the war, but the scope of her character is revealed when she sees that Menelaus and his guests are distressing themselves with reminiscences, and mixes a drug which she has brought from Egypt and which deadens pain and sorrow (4.219 ff.). She has learned from her sufferings, and the tenderness which is already hers in the *Iliad* is turned to new purposes.

Odysseus himself in the *Odyssey* is an enlarged and elaborated version of what he is in the *Iliad*. His main qualities there are cunning and endurance. He keeps his head when others lose theirs, notably after Agamemnon's ill-judged test of the army's morale (ii 166 ff.). He is throughout a notable leader, resourceful and brave. In the *Odyssey*, where he is far longer on the stage, some of his qualities are turned in new directions. First, his cunning is tested in unfamiliar conditions, as in the cave of the Cyclops, where he takes on some qualities of a folk-hero and sustains them quite convincingly. Secondly, his need for cunning is enforced by his own recklessness. It is his fault that he is trapped in the cave of the Cyclops, since he has insisted on entering it, and equally it is his fault that he seeks out Circe's dwelling by himself. Thirdly, his abundant appetites, known from his taste for food and drink in the *Iliad*, are extended in the *Odyssey* to living with Circe and with Calypso, not perhaps in entire satisfaction but still competently. Lastly, the warrior of the *Iliad* becomes the returned wanderer of the *Odyssey* and needs all his powers of decision, command and improvisation. These he amply displays. The man who strikes Thersites and kills Dolon is not likely to spare the Suitors or the servants, male and female, who have worked for them. Odysseus in the *Odyssey* is a magnified version of Odysseus in the *Iliad*, but he remains substantially the same man and recognizable in his main being.

Finally, there are in the *Odyssey* two passages where Homer presents ghosts of the dead, and each includes some chief figures of the *Iliad*. At 11.385–567 Odysseus, at the end of the world, summons ghosts with an offering of blood, and among those who appear are Agamemnon, Achilles and Aias. All three have died since the end of the *Iliad*. Agamemnon has been murdered by his wife, in marked contrast with Odysseus, whose faithful Penelope holds out bravely against the Suitors. His story emphasizes the dangers that await those who return from Troy, but sheds no new light on his personality. Aias, in a brief appearance, adds a new dimension to his simple character in the *Iliad*, for in the interval he has killed himself because his honour has been wounded by Odysseus. Odysseus does his best to appease him, but Aias takes no notice and makes no answer. The most striking figure is Achilles, for his words complement by contrast what he says in Book ix when momentarily he rejects the heroic life. Now he knows what he has lost, for he would rather 'work on the land as the serf of a man with no property, with no great means of life, than reign over all the perished dead' (11.489–91). His only consolation is to know that his son Neoptolemus is already a stout warrior (11.540). These three ghosts form a link with the *Iliad*, and when Odysseus speaks to them he speaks to his peers, as he does nowhere else in the *Odyssey*.

More mysterious is 24.1–204, where the ghosts of the Suitors are escorted by Hermes to the land of the dead and met by some heroes of the *Iliad*, notably Achilles and Agamemnon. Though the passage is thought to be a later addition, at least it has a part in the whole plan of the *Odyssey*. Achilles hears of his own death and funeral from Agamemnon (24.36 ff.); at it the Muses sang and the ceremony is a fitting climax to a heroic life. To this the Suitors present a complete antithesis. Their ignominious deaths are the proper end to their squalid careers. In this passage the poet seems to have aimed at more than one effect. First, when he makes Agamemnon say that Odysseus is indeed fortunate to have a wife like Penelope (24.192 ff.) and very unlike Clytaemnestra, he emphasizes a subsidiary theme of the *Odyssey*, but does not gain much by it. Secondly, the parade of the ghosts of Troy, in which Patroclus, Aias and Antilochus are named as well as Achilles and Agamemnon (24.16–17), provides a final curtain for great figures of the *Iliad* and of the heroic age. Their place here recalls them at the end of a long story, and the renewed attention paid to them brings various themes together in a last bow. Thirdly, there is a real contrast between the death and glory of Achilles, immortalized in song, and the miserable careers of the Suitors, who are at the other extreme from the true nobility of the heroic ideal. Whoever composed this passage, must have felt that the *Odyssey* must be brought into contact with the *Iliad*, and this he did by stressing what real heroes are.

When we look at the structure of the *Odyssey*, Books 1–4 look as if they could be omitted by bards who were pressed for time and wished to plunge *in medias res* with the more thrilling adventures of Odysseus, but this does not mean that these books do not serve a dramatic purpose. In fact they serve more than one. First, they show the general plight of Ithaca and the particular plight of Penelope in the absence of Odysseus. This is indispensable to any understanding of his difficulties on his return and of the character of the Suitors, from whom he is to exact vengeance. It is bad enough that they should harry his wife and devour his substance and corrupt his servants, but they soon put themselves brutally in the wrong by plotting the death of Telemachus. In this situation everything turns on the possible return of Odysseus. The poet shows how little is known of him, how anticipations of his return vary between irrational hope and not impossible despair. This creates the suspense at which the poet excels. It is to some extent lessened when Telemachus gets news of Odysseus from Menelaus, but it remains vague and unsubstantiated, though omens and portents suggest that something is going to happen. These books build up a growing assurance in the return of Odysseus, and incidentally introduce the other characters with whom he will be associated. The *Odyssey* can be imagined without them, but they add to its range and richness and do much to set its plot to work.

Books 1–4 do more than this. They prepare the way for much that comes later. For instance, Telemachus is cast for a large part, and is not yet ready for it. But he begins to face his responsibilities and to test his powers. His access of courage takes the Suitors by surprise (1.381–2; 2.85–6), and before long they are sufficiently afraid of him to plot his death. By this means he becomes an important participant in the action, and he gives sturdy help in the vengeance. Again, these books anticipate in their manner the dual nature of the *Odyssey*, its element of domestic comedy and its element of fable and fancy. The first is to the fore here, and has a special charm. This manner is unadventurous and unexciting, but its human normality presents a fine contrast with the gluttonous revels and gross manners of the Suitors. Against this are set the stories told by Telemachus' hosts at Sparta, which take us either back to the heroic world of Troy, as when Helen tells how she recognized Odysseus when he came disguised as a beggar to spy in Troy (4.240–64), or forward to the world of marvels, as when Menelaus tells how he tricked Proteus, the old man of the sea, into revealing the fate of Odysseus (4.351 ff.). The main notes of the *Odyssey* are struck at the start, and in due course each is taken up to make its contribution to the whole design.

The middle section of the *Odyssey*, Books 5–12, has a notably distinctive character. Though its more extravagant actions are told by Odysseus himself, the first part, his departure from Calypso and his arrival and welcome in Phaeacia, are told in the third person with an outstanding objectivity, in which Odysseus emerges in all his gifts and dominates the scene. These books provide a skilful transition to the wonders that follow. The events are not yet marvellous, nor are there any monsters. Odysseus shows his physical powers by swimming in a rough sea for two days and two nights, and his resourcefulness by winning the help of the Phaeacian royal family. Yet Phaeacia is not real in the same sense as Ithaca. The seasons allow crops all the year round; the servants in the palace are made of metal by Hephaestus; the Phaeacians hardly mingle with other peoples and are consciously proud of their singularity; unlike authentic heroes they live not for war but for dance and song. Once Odysseus has arrived and been handsomely welcomed, we are ready to hear of the wilder wonders which he is about to tell. In Phaeacia these seem less improbable than in Ithaca, and the lively entertainment in Phaeacia prepares us for what lies outside the known world. At the start we have even left the sea, but it is soon present again when Odysseus tells his tale.

Even at this stage, and still more in the narrative of Odysseus, it is clear that the poet is familiar with different versions of a tale and has to make his choice between them. This is easy enough when Odysseus meets Nausicaa. The theme of Wanderer meeting the king's daughter is old and widely spread. A less human version is known from Egypt. A man is shipwrecked on an island. He finds it rich in fruit and trees, and is royally entertained, loaded with gifts and given a safe passage home to Egypt. But his hostess is a snake, thirty ells long, and her family is like her. She treats the castaway with much kindness and courtesy; this is a primitive version of the Nausicaa story, which has not yet assumed its fully human character.[1] The episode in the *Odyssey* shows no misfits or oddities, and looks like a complete tale, but it

[1] L. Radermacher, *Die Erzählungen der Odyssee*, Vienna, 1915, pp. 38-47.

may well have grown from humble origins. What is remarkable is that while Homer hints at a story in which the Wanderer marries the Princess, the Egyptian tale suggests nothing of the kind. So the treatment of Nausicaa by Odysseus has an ancient precedent. In this case variants have been absorbed into a final version, and Homer's choice was forced upon him by Odysseus' destiny to be joined again to Penelope.

In their long and widely scattered careers such tales develop variations, and the poet has to choose between alternatives. This is very much the case with the Cyclops. As the *Odyssey* tells it, the substantial, unchanged element is that the hero and his companion are caught in the cave of a one-eyed cannibal giant, and after suffering losses in their own number blind him and escape. This story occurs in many countries and is clearly primordial. Homer knew more than one version and made his own choice. First, there is the trick by which Odysseus says that his name is 'No-man', and so when the Cyclops calls for help and says 'No-man is hurting me' (9.408), his friends go away. The trick throve happily in other contexts, but is well in place here. To set the Cyclops among other monsters of his kind makes him more formidable and increases the danger to Odysseus; the trick saves him at a critical point. Second, the Cyclops is blinded with a stake lying in the cave which is not yet ready for use. That is why the Cyclops will not take it with him when he goes out, and Odysseus can use it to blind him. The Cyclops eats his visitors raw after breaking their heads on the floor like puppies (9.289–90). This is perhaps more bestial than to cook them first, and since there is no need for a spit, the stake takes its place. Thirdly, in the escape from the cave there is one version in which Odysseus and his companions kill the ram and the sheep, clothe themselves in their skins, and behave like them as they walk out on all fours. But the Homeric version brings advantages, notably when the ram goes out, with Odysseus under its belly, and we are simultaneously afraid that the Cyclops will catch the escapers and touched by his affectionate words to the ram. Choices between competing versions had to be made, and were, usually with good results.

The episode of Circe, which reads very easily, contains traces of competing versions. She is a witch, daughter of the sun, who lives in a stone palace among woods on an otherwise uninhabited island. This is common form, and suggests her dangerous character. In such stories the adventurer is guided to her by some chance, and behind the story in the *Odyssey* we may discern a stag who did the guiding. Odysseus meets such a stag but kills it and with some effort carries it to his companions for their supper (10.156 ff.). Then having seen the palace, he decides to send a party to investigate. He does not go himself or take the lead, but divides his crew into two companies, one of which is chosen by lot to go. This procedure creates suspense and leaves Odysseus free to take action later and remedy the evils that have befallen the first party. This party finds wolves and lions which greet it in a friendly way, and are in fact men transformed by Circe. But this is their only appearance. When the companions are turned back into men from swine, nothing is said about these earlier victims. Their function is to reveal something sinister in Circe's dwelling, and when they have done that, they are forgotten. When Odysseus' companions are turned into swine, we are expressly told that they keep their wits as before (10.240), and this is not usual in this kind of theme, where the witch tends to instil forgetfulness of former lives. We may guess why Homer does what he does. He has already dealt with the theme of forgetfulness in telling of the Lotus-eaters, who forget all about their return home (9.94–7), and the theme is not suitable for repetition. Finally, on his way to Circe Odysseus meets Hermes, who tells him of the danger ahead and gives him a plant, *moly*, to protect him from Circe's spells. The plant is carefully described, and then we hear no more. We do not know how Odysseus uses it, or how it works; what we do know is that Circe's spells have no effect on him. In these ways Homer keeps the episode of Circe simple and circumvents obstacles in the tradition.

In the passage of years a traditional theme may assume new shapes, which are so different that they are really new tales. The *Odyssey* deals twice with the ancient theme of the witch who detains the hero on his return by making him live with her. She need not be malevolent but she hinders his desire to go home. In the *Odyssey* she appears in two quite different forms, as Circe and Calypso. If Circe, who has a ruthless, cruel side, is the Hawk, Calypso is the Concealer, who keeps Odysseus hidden on Ogygia for eight years. Both live alone on remote islands, in circumstances of some beauty. Yet, allowing for this degree of likeness, the differences are great. Circe is subdued by the superior cunning and courage of Odysseus, and after admitting her defeat, welcomes him as her lover; Calypso saves him from the sea after shipwreck and her devotion to him is complete. Circe keeps Odysseus for a year and then releases him without complaint; Calypso keeps him for eight years, hoping to make him immortal but is told by the gods to give him up, which she does unhappily but graciously. Circe at the start has a sinister glamour; there is nothing sinister in Calypso. The two are distinct and distinguishable, but we can see why both are needed. The adventure with Circe is exciting for its own sake and entirely appropriate to the hero on his wanderings; the sojourn with Calypso has much charm and beauty but lacks dramatic variety. It is needed to fill a gap in the story. After his ten years of war at Troy Odysseus is away from home for another ten years before he returns to Ithaca. By the time of his shipwreck and the loss of all his companions only ten years have passed, and the remaining eight have to be accounted for. Homer does this by confining him to Calypso's island, where nothing can be heard of him and his fate remains a mystery to his family and his friends, and is almost forgotten by the gods.

Circe begins as a malevolent witch, but once Odysseus has subdued her, she becomes his helper and shows no signs of her sinister past. She then takes up another part which may belong to her original character—she foretells the future and gives advice about it. That heroes should have this happen is common enough, but Homer seems to have been faced by two traditional characters who prophesy. Circe is one, but she insists that Odysseus should consult the other—the ghost of the seer Tiresias.

This is a very ancient theme and bears some resemblance to *Gilgamesh*, where the hero crosses the waters of death to consult Uta-Napishtim. Odysseus sails to the edge of the world and calls up the ghost of Tiresias, who says very little about the immediate future, except in warning him not to eat the cattle of the Sun in Thrinacia (11.104 ff.), but gives him a precise forecast of his last days and quiet ending (11.121ff.), with advice on the ritual that will appease Poseidon. We may perhaps assume that in earlier versions Tiresias said more than this, and that his warning about the cattle is only part of a set of warnings and forecasts. But Homer transfers these to Circe. When Odysseus comes back to her, she gives him a careful forecast of the dangers that lie before him (12.37–141). This device keeps Circe still powerful, even if she has reformed her habits, but at the cost of a lengthy prevision of what will come soon afterwards. It all happens according to plan, but lacks the element of surprise.

In Books 13–24 we are back in Ithaca and a familiar world. Yet here too the main actions are derived largely from folk-tale, and old themes exploited with novelty. At some point the Wanderer must be recognized. No doubt there were many versions of this, and the recognition need not all come at once. Homer moves through a series of recognitions, each separate and distinct, and each marking a step forward. The first is when Odysseus, transformed into a shrunken old beggar is for a short time given back his old shape and reveals himself to Telemachus (16.166 ff.). Athene makes it possible, and to that degree it is supernatural. What matters is that Odysseus must not start on his vengeance entirely alone, and his obvious companion is his son, who stays with him for the rest of the poem. The second recognition is a stroke of genius. When Odysseus arrives at his palace, he sees lying in his midden outside the gates his dog Argos, whom he trained twenty years before. The dog is neglected and full of ticks, but he wags his tail and drops his ears and struggles towards his old master (17.291–304). Odysseus knows him at once and says a few words about him, and then the dog dies 'having seen Odysseus again in the twentieth year' (17.327). This recognition is based on affection and loyalty and conveys swiftly, and surely how Odysseus belongs to Ithaca and how deep his roots there are. The third comes when Odysseus has his feet washed by his old nurse, Euryclea. It is dark, and Penelope is sitting in the shadow not far away. The nurse recognizes a scar which Odysseus got long ago on a boar-hunt, and is on the point of crying out, when the basin of water is upset and Odysseus puts his hand on her throat and enjoins her silence (19.386 ff.). This is the most dramatic of the recognitions, and the one in which the scar, used twice elsewhere, really creates a situation. Through it the recognition by Penelope is postponed until it can be most effective. In the fourth recognition, during the fight in the hall, Odysseus reveals himself to Eumaeus, who accepts his word and, like the nurse, recognizes the scar, but without any exciting reaction (21.207 ff.). Fifth is the recognition by Penelope, and this is the most unexpected. The signs that have satisfied others do not satisfy her, and she tries to test the stranger by telling Euryclea to make a bed, but the stranger knows that Penelope and he have their own special, secret bed made out of an olive-trunk in the heart of the palace. This is highly appropriate, as Odysseus and Penelope are man and wife and the bed is an intimate sign of it. Finally, Odysseus goes off to see his old father Laertes in the country and identifies himself first by the scar (24.331 ff.) and then by knowing the details of Laertes' orchard which he helped to plant. All these recognitions have a certain simplicity. If the scar does the most work, that is perhaps because it comes from the oldest tradition, while the dog Argos, who needs no sign, looks as if he were Homer's own invention. The accumulation of six recognitions suggests that there were many variants in the tradition, and that Homer gave a subordinate purpose to some which might have been of primary importance in earlier versions.

Somewhat different from the recognitions are two events which do not reveal the identity of the Wanderer but show that he is someone remarkable. These are the stringing of the great bow which Odysseus left behind when he went to Troy (21.39), and the exhibition-shot with it through a line of axes planted in the

ground.[1] It is conceivable that in earlier versions the two events
were alternative and that either of them would suffice to prove
who Odysseus is. Nor must we assume that, once the bow had
been strung, the slaughter of the Suitors followed immediately. The
Odyssey finds its climax in the combination of these events, but it
is possible that originally neither event served just this purpose.
The stringing of the bow may have been no more than a test of
the Wanderer's identity, proposed by his wife, who is still not sure
of him. So the exhibition-shot may have come from some other
context, as when the Suitors compete for marriage with Penelope,
and even then Odysseus need not take a part. In its present place it
establishes his preeminence, and leaves him with the bow in his
hands as an instrument for vengeance.

When a story belongs to a cycle centred on some main point,
it may not fit in easily with others in a like position. Tradition is
aware of its place, and the poet may feel that he owes it some
attention, but it may lead to difficulties and to some awkwardness
in his main scheme. This is the case, in the *Odyssey*, with the shroud
which Penelope claims to be weaving for Laertes when he dies.
She tells the Suitors that when it is finished, she will make her choice
among them, but every night she undoes the work of the day,
until a point comes when the Suitors catch her at it and know that
she is deceiving them (2.85–110). We can see the story behind this.
The shroud is a device to put off a decision as long as possible, and
and as such Penelope reports it to the unrecognized Odysseus
(19.136 ff.). The theme is not in itself very conclusive, and the
discovery of Penelope's trickery by the Suitors does not force the
issue of her marriage as we might expect. There was moreover a
different version, which appears when the ghost of Amphimedon
says that when Penelope finished the shroud, 'in that hour an evil
spirit brought Odysseus from somewhere to the border of the
land' (24.146–50). This comes from the suspicious conclusion of
the *Odyssey*, but its author uses good and independent material;
for this is just what the trick of the shroud should have done.
Homer must have known it and rejected it for his own less

---

[1] It is still not clear how exactly this is done.

emphatic version because he did not wish Penelope's marriage to be confused with the return of Odysseus, and because he wished this return to be both prolonged and secret.

Another slightly inconclusive theme is that of the seer Theoclymenus. When Telemachus is about to sail from Pylos, Theoclymenus suddenly appears and asks for protection, since he is guilty of murder. Telemachus takes him on board (15.256–81). On arriving in Ithaca Theoclymenus asks where he is to stay, and Telemachus, rather strangely, says with Eurymachus, who is one of the Suitors and a prominent enemy. This conveys the depressed and defeated mood of Telemachus. At this point a hawk flies overhead carrying a dove, and Theoclymenus interprets this as an omen of success, with the result that Telemachus changes his mind and gives other orders for the reception of Theoclymenus (15.525 ff.). Later, at the palace, Theoclymenus meets Penelope and tells her with full assurance that Odysseus is already in his own country and plotting evil for the Suitors (17.152–61). As a seer he knows this from the omen of the hawk and the dove. Finally, when the doom of the Suitors is near and one of them has just thrown an ox's foot at Odysseus, they are seized with a frenzy of madness, and Theoclymenus in ringing tones foresees their doom (20.345–57). It is an apocalyptic moment, but it is the last for Theoclymenus. He has done his task, which is to forecast events by augury and vision, but we suspect that in some other version he must have done more, that he may have played a more prominent part in letting Penelope know of her husband's presence or in driving the Suitors to their destruction. The element of the supernatural which he represents adds something to the story but is not fully exploited.

In these loose ends and imperfectly exploited themes we can see traces of the different variants which Homer must have known and from which he had to make his selection. But this is not the problem with the end of the *Odyssey* from 23.297 to 24.548. Here there are indeed unexpected contradictions, and there is perhaps an explanation of them. The two great Alexandrian scholars, Aristarchus and Aristophanes, regarded 23.296, 'Then they came gladly to the place of their old bed', as the 'end' or the

'limit' of the *Odyssey*. We do not know why they thought this.
They may conceivably have had external evidence that some good
manuscripts ended at this point, or they may have made their
decision on the strength of anomalies of language and narrative
after this point. We cannot dismiss their view, nor can we deny
that in some ways the 'continuation' differs in some ways from the
rest of the poem, not merely in linguistic solecisms but in actual
episodes, like Penelope's web. It is unlikely that the main poet of
the *Odyssey* composed this part, but that does not deprive it of all
significance. At least it shows how the Homeric manner persisted
with adaptations, and how someone felt that the end of the
Odyssey called for some sort of epilogue.

The *Odyssey* might, in our view, have had a perfectly satis-
factory end when Odysseus and Penelope go to bed at 23.296. But
someone must have felt that more should be said, and we may ask
what advantages, if any, were gained by adding the last passages.
Odysseus gives Penelope an account of his adventures, tactfully
omitting his infidelities. The audience hardly needs this, and we
could assume that Penelope will get the story sooner or later.
The appearance of the Suitors in Hades indicates their inferiority
to the men of Troy, but not much is made of this, and what is
stressed is the comparison between Clytaemnestra and Penelope,
which the audience might make for itself. On the other hand the
recognition of Odysseus by Laertes has a quiet charm and shows
Odysseus in a playful, teasing mood. It is family poetry, and there
is something to be said for making Odysseus meet his father after
he has met his son and his wife. Moreover the fight between the
supporters of Odysseus and the kinsmen of the Suitors indicates
that the slaying was not as final as it seemed, and it may have
provided a start for new adventures in which Odysseus leaves
Ithaca, as he seems to have done in the *Telegony*. The continuation
serves no clear single purpose, but suggests a poet who would like
to prolong the story in various ways for different reasons. He may
have used old material, at least in Penelope's web, and he has a gift
for quiet narrative in the scene with Laertes. Otherwise we miss the
swing and the strength of the main poem.

The sources of the *Odyssey* are different from those of the *Iliad* and the difference explains some of its character. If it deals with marvels and monsters, so to a smaller extent does the *Iliad*. In both poems gods interfere with the course of nature. When Aphrodite spirits Paris away from the battlefield (iii 380) or protects Aeneas (v. 315–17), it is not very different from when Athene covers Odysseus with a mist in Phaeacia (7.15) or changes his appearance to prevent him being recognized (13.430–3). Though the *Iliad* contains the remarkable scene when the horse of Achilles speaks to him, it is because Hera has for this one occasion given it a human voice (xix 407 ff.), and this is well within the power of the gods. The *Odyssey* differs when its marvels are not caused by the gods but belong to the world of legend. The wind-bag of Aeolus, the transformations of Circe, the summoning of ghosts at the end of the world, the monstrosity of Scylla, are outside human experience and do not belong to the strictly heroic world of the *Iliad*. In face of them Odysseus conducts himself heroically, as when he insists on hearing the Sirens' song but forestalls disaster by getting himself lashed to the mast (12.178–9). But the monsters which he has to face are outside both human and heroic experience.

Homer evidently saw this and tried to bring his monsters as near as possible to humanity, to relate them to it, and even in some degree to humanize them. This is certainly the case with the Cyclops, who despite his single eye, his bulk 'like a wooded peak of tall mountains' (9.190–2), and his cannibalistic gluttony, is made real by his pastoral life, by his care for his flocks, by his affection for his ram. He is hideous and horrible, but not outside comprehension. Comparable in some respects to him is the queen of the Laestrygonians. She lives in a rocky fjord, and all looks easy until the scouts of Odysseus entering her palace, 'saw a woman as big as a mountain-peak, and they hated her' (10.113). She grabs one of them and plans to make her supper of him. She is of the same loathsome breed as the Cyclops, but since he has recently received full treatment, she is deftly conveyed in a short sketch. The Sirens, despite their gift of song which lures men to death and the bones of decaying bodies round them (12.45–6), are careful to do no more than invite Odysseus to listen to them on the latest subjects of song (12.184–92). The exception to this realism is Scylla, who is a monster among monsters, aptly and fully described, with her twelve feet, her six necks, each with a head and three rows of teeth (12.89–91); she seizes six men from the ship of Odysseus and eats them while they are still crying for help and stretching out their hands, so that Odysseus comments:

'That was the most piteous thing that I saw with my eyes of all that I suffered searching out the ways of the sea.' (12.258–9)

Scylla must be descended from tales of sea-monsters, of giant krakens and man-slaying cuttle-fish, and perhaps because she has some basis in fact Homer feels that he must describe her exactly. She is far from ordinary, and yet one small touch brings her into the compass of living things—her voice is like that of a puppy (12.86). It is quite unexpected and almost absurd, and it is just this that brings it home. The monsters of the *Odyssey* are clearly visualized. Their horror comes not from vagueness but from clearly imagined actions and the menace of a horrible death which they offer. The only approximation to them in the *Iliad* is the Chimaera:

It was a divine creature, not of human race, in front a lion, in the rear a snake, and in the middle a goat, and it breathed the terrible strength of flaming fire. (vi 180–2)

Description is reduced to the barest essentials, but the Chimaera emerges clearly. This is the Homeric way of looking at monsters, and it is fully developed in the *Odyssey*. It is quite different from the shapeless horrors which the long northern night gives to its dragons.

This controlling realism informs most parts of the *Odyssey* and gives much of its special flavour. It accounts for a certain quiet poetry which is not very noticeable in the *Iliad*, but makes the *Odyssey* friendly and familiar. It finds poetry in quite unassuming and humble subjects, as when Telemachus goes to bed and Euryclea folds his clothes and hangs them on a peg (1.439–40), or his

33. *Part woman, part hound, part serpent, the monster Scylla* ABOVE *of the* Odyssey *is shown below a crab on a silver coin of the fifth century*
34. *An archaic bronze of one of Odysseus' companions escaping from the cave of Polyphemus under a ram* (see p. 125)

35, 36. *Hardly a conversation piece between Penelope and her son Telemachus, but, framed by her loom, this drawing on a skyphos of* c. 450 B.C. *illustrates perfectly the legend of the faithful, patient wife (see pp. 122, 160).* BELOW: *from a pot of the same period, Odysseus dismays the suitors before slaying them with his bow (see p. 130)*

ship sets out in the evening and the wind fills the sail and the dark waves resound about the stern (2.427–9). Life in the palace, despite the disruption caused by the Suitors, follows a routine, and there is a quiet dignity in the reception of guests, the laying out of tables, the scrubbing of them with sponges. In making his raft Odysseus shows a high technical accomplishment, and the mere making has its own interest. It was this that Racine admired so greatly, when he compared its language with Latin:

Calypso lui donne encore un vilebrequin et des clous, tant Homère est exact à décrire les moindres particularités, ce qui a bonne grace dans le grec, au lieu que le latin est beaucoup plus réservé, et ne s'amuse pas à de si petites choses.[1]

Yet, though the Homeric language can say anything that it likes and not lose its force, that is because the poetical vision for which it works is so direct and straightforward. It finds interest and charm everywhere, and is happy to say so.

The same kind of realism can be seen in the characters. We have marked how Odysseus is developed from his old self in the *Iliad*, but he is the only character of any complexity, and that is because legend insisted upon a more than common personality. The others go their own way, and make their individual mark. At the start Telemachus is only a boy, and conscious of it. But he wishes to assert himself, even though he lacks the authority and the experience to do so. His voyage to Pylos makes a man of him. On it he settles his own decisions, and, when he comes back to Ithaca, he is ready for action, and follows and helps his father. Penelope presents rather a special problem. Legend marked her as prudent, and she has kept the Suitors off for ten years, not merely by the stratagem of the web but by other postponements and evasions. Despite long hours of tearful lamentation for her lost husband she keeps her courage, and her sudden appearances among the Suitors reduce them to momentary acquiescence, which cannot all be ascribed to good manners. Her prudence makes her suspicious, and that is why she is so slow to recognize Odysseus as her

[1] J. Racine, *Oeuvres complètes*, ed. Pléiade, II pp. 755–6.

husband. She and Telemachus are supported by the swineherd
Eumaeus and the old nurse Euryclea, and though the first claim of
these is their unswerving loyalty to their master, they display an
innate nobility in their response to the demands made of them.
The party of Odysseus on Ithaca is homogeneous in that it is held
together by loyalty to him and hatred of the Suitors. It contains no
very powerful personality except the great man himself, but its
members are sufficiently distinctive to set him in a full perspective.

The Suitors are beyond dispute deplorable, not in the plebeian
way of Thersites but as a degenerate corruption of heroes. They
have a high opinion of themselves and no scruples about getting
what they want. Antinous differs from Eurymachus only in being
more outspokenly brutal. The others conform to type, except
perhaps Amphinomus, who has some relics of decency but
does not escape death because of them (22.89–94). Their deaths
are deserved, as are those of the household of Odysseus who
follow them. The beggar Irus, the goatherd Melanthius, the
serving-woman Melantho, begin by insulting the unrecognized
Odysseus and come to suitable ends. In the Suitors it is hard not
to see an embodiment of a heroic society in decay. This is the
generation that did not fight at Troy, and their lack of heroic
qualities fits the relatively unheroic temper of the *Odyssey*. It
makes little attempt to maintain the lofty level of the *Iliad*, and the
hero who holds it together is never matched by anyone of his own
calibre. Even Alcinous, despite his wealth and kingly condescen-
sion, is not heroic, and some of his court, notably Laodamas and
Euryalus, lack proper courtesy (8.132 ff.). This lower tone comes
partly from the material of the *Odyssey*, which is concerned not
with heroic prowess in war but with wild adventures and a
cunning vengeance. It is significant that, when Odysseus kills the
Suitors, he has every advantage over them, and though this is due
to his foresight, it is not the way in which Achilles would take on
an enemy.

In the *Iliad* the intermittent interventions of the gods and the
frivolity of some of their actions provide a contrast to the dangers
and destructiveness of heroic life; in the *Odyssey* such a contrast is

not needed, and the gods are treated with a different intention. The nearest approximation to the spirit of the Deception of Zeus is the song of Demodocus about Ares and Aphrodite (8.266–366), but its purpose is to provide relief before Odysseus starts on the tale of his adventures, and incidentally to throw light on the Phaeacians, who, having no heroic obligations or challenges, are well served by this kind of song. Otherwise the *Odyssey* treats the gods less freely than the *Iliad* and in a more calculated way. They are concerned with human actions, and the council on Olympus, which decides to do something about Odysseus, keeps an eye on such wrongdoing as the behaviour of Aegisthus (1.32–41). Poseidon is entirely justified in maintaining his wrath against Odysseus for blinding Polyphemus (1.20–1), which leads to his being wrecked on his raft, and incidentally to the ship of the Phaeacians, which takes him to Ithaca, being turned to stone (13.163–4). But apart from these special cases, the dominating part played by the gods in the *Odyssey* is the friendship between Athene and Odysseus. This recalls such occasions in the *Iliad* as when, in the panic after Agamemnon's false proposal to withdraw from Troy, Athene sets Odysseus to restore order (ii 173–82) or on night-operations keeps an eye on him (x 245, 277, 482, 497). In the *Odyssey* she is seldom far away. Both on Phaeacia and in Ithaca she is a constant helper and gives Odysseus advice and practical assistance, while in the intervals she instils confidence into his son. She even takes part in the slaughter of the Suitors by deflecting weapons aimed at Odysseus (22.256, 273) and frightening the Suitors by flashing her aegis from the roof (22.297–8). Her character as a virgin-goddess makes it impossible for her to be in love with Odysseus but she holds him in great affection and admiration. They treat each other on equal terms, as when she praises him for his cunning (13.291 ff.), or he recalls her kindness to him at Troy (13.314). The Homeric poems have no parallel to so close a companionship between a goddess and a mortal, and though later Greek literature occasionally allows such friendships, it makes much less of them than Homer does of this. It enhances the position of Odysseus as a heroic survivor in an unheroic world. A man of this quality deserves the affection and the support of the gods.

In general the *Odyssey* lacks the sustained splendour of the *Iliad*, has fewer overwhelming moments and a less demanding conception of human worth. The slaughter of the Suitors provides a thrilling climax but lacks the profound pathos of the death of Hector, while the cold, vengeful anger of Odysseus is not comparable to the fiery, devouring passion of Achilles. All is set in a lower key, and this may be due to the nature of the subject and the traditional treatment of it. Folk-tales and fairy-tales, even tales of injured wives and revengeful husbands, need not summon the same powers as the wounded pride of Achilles or the fate of Troy. The *Odyssey* has moments of breathless excitement and moving pathos, but its normal level is less stirring and closer to ordinary experience. Even if tradition was partly responsible for setting this tone, there may be an additional reason for it in the poet's desire to compose a poem nearer to the life that he knew and to the events of every day. By combining these with impossible adventures and enthralling marvels he could set them in a new and brighter light. 'Longinus' thinks that this difference between the *Iliad* and the *Odyssey* is due to the poet's advancing years, and he makes a good observation when he says:

Accordingly, in the *Odyssey* Homer may be compared to the setting sun, whose greatness remains without its intensity. He does not here maintain so high a level as in those poems of Ilium. His sublimities are not even sustained and free from sinking; there is not the same profusion of passions one after another, nor the supple and public style, packed with inventions drawn from real life. (*On the Sublime* 9.13)

'Longinus' assumes that both poems were composed by the same author, and that is something we shall discuss later. For the moment it is enough to assume that they have marked differences, but these can conceivably be ascribed either to a difference of kind established by tradition or to the difference of outlook and temper which a single poet may develop with the advance of years.

APPENDIX

BOOK 11 of the *Odyssey* presents problems of a special kind. Its theme, the visit of the hero to the edge of the world where he calls up the dead, is not ultimately different from the visit of Gilgamesh to Uta-Napishtim to enquire how to avoid death. A theme of this kind was specially exposed to dangers of interpolation to suit religious views, which are not strictly relevant to the story. This certainly seems to be the case with Book 11. The main structure is clear. Odysseus digs a trench and fills it with blood, which draws the ghosts. Those who drink of it regain their wits and speak to him. The first section ends with the incomparable scene between Odysseus and the ghost of his mother. Then comes a long passage, 225–332, in which a series of famous heroines appear, drink and are questioned by Odysseus. Each receives a few lively, dramatic lines, but the narrative is in the third person and Odysseus himself plays no part, while the heroines do not speak for themselves. The method of narration is quite different from what precedes and we may with reason think that the whole passage is an addition, which has nothing to do with Odysseus but profits from the presence of ghosts to tell some short biographies in a Hesiodic manner. After it there is an interval, in which Alcinous questions Odysseus (11.333–76), and then Odysseus resumes his tale in his first manner in a series of interviews with famous ghosts (ibid. 377–567), ending dramatically with the silence of the injured Aias. This is a good end to the heroes, and we would be happy if the passage stopped here. But in 568–629 the poet tells how Odysseus sees first Minos, judging the quarrels of the dead, and Orion, and then the three great sinners, Tityus, Tantalus, and Sisyphus, suffering their punishments. Since Odysseus is above the earth, there is a real and flagrant contradiction, for it presupposes that Odysseus is in Hades and sees what is there. These sinners do not belong to the Homeric world, but to the world of religious reform and speculation in the sixth century, and we can well understand that some reformer got the lines into the *Odyssey* when its text was neither settled nor secure. It is odd that they begin with Orion, 572–5, who is seen hunting, but is not a great sinner, and end with Heracles, 601–27, who ought to be on Olympus but is here represented by a phantom. It is hard to surmise why these two figures precede and follow the sinners, but the whole interpolation is so inept that we can only lay the blame for it on some poet who wished to bring the underworld up to date.

CHAPTER EIGHT

The Poetry of Action

THE *Iliad* and the *Odyssey* are preeminently poems of action. Their first purpose is to engage the hearers in what happens, to involve them imaginatively in it. In this respect they resemble not only other heroic poetry but much oral narrative verse which may be sub-heroic or shamanistic. Their main objective can be paralleled in ancient poems like *Gilgamesh* and in modern ones like the Kirghiz *Manas*. In such poems the thrill of action comes first but is attended by much else, notably by a concern for what human beings do and suffer and the many ways in which they face their challenges. In heroic poetry this is all-important because without it the mere account of violent behaviour would pall even for the most assiduous addict and lose much of its significance by its neglect of human feelings and considerations. In the Homeric poems the action is wonderfully varied, and though we know in general what is going to come next, we seldom know exactly how it will come. Surprise is never lacking and sharpens an endless range of effects.

Though the strong dramatic quality of the Homeric poems arises from action, it often goes beyond it and touches on the character of the actors, their thoughts and their feelings as their words reveal them. Speeches, even soliloquies, abound and add an element of drama, which is woven closely into the narrative and wins attention by its advance beyond mere action to the motives that prompt it. In this respect, there emerges what may be called a lyrical spirit, partly in dealing with nature whether directly in descriptions or indirectly in similes, and partly in presenting powerful emotions such as affection or grief. Both of these classes would, if expressed in the first person, inspire lyrical poems, but in Homer they are indispensable to the narrative and to its human rise and fall. Even contemplative poetry, which assumed an unashamedly didactic form with Hesiod and made possible the first outbreaks into philosophy, occurs in both poems in general considerations advanced by the characters. Odysseus' comments on the shameless demands of an empty belly (7.216–21) have their counterpart at a much higher level in what Achilles says to Priam about the way in which the gods apportion good and bad to men (xxiv 527–33). Such generalizations help the audience to understand what is happening, but through the mouths of the characters and not of the poet. They do not break the general objectivity of heroic narrative, but make the characters more real by giving their underlying views on human life. These thoughts arise from the action, and are less a comment on it than an actual part of it.

The heroic poet does not normally assert his own opinions or pass judgments on what happens. Perhaps he is not of sufficient social standing to lay down the law to an audience which may include the local rulers; perhaps the effort of heroic poetry to attain a self-contained life of its own excludes personal intrusions which interfere with the story. In either case the rule is generally followed. Homer reveals himself in the nature and quality of his creation; he does not attempt to guide our reactions to them. His independence from his work may be illustrated by a small point in which he allows himself a small comment on what happens. He often uses the word *nēpios*, which means, in colloquial English, 'poor', with often some slight suggestion of 'silly'. It is applied to Patroclus when he asks Achilles to send him to battle (xvi 46), and there Homer explains that his request is really for death. Telemachus uses it of himself, with special reference to his boyhood when he did not know how to deal with the Suitors (2.313; 18.229; 20.310). In these cases we may discern understanding and compassion, and also perhaps in the use of the word for the companions of Odysseus when they court doom by eating the cattle of the Sun (1.8) or linger disastrously in the land of the

Ciconians (9.44). The word suggests that men sometimes act as children and pay for it. It is a small indication of what Homer feels for his characters, of his tenderness for them in their mistakes, but it is not a judgment, still less a condemnation. His characters stand in their own right and do what they do without Homer's comments.

This is not to say that he has not his preferences and distastes among them, but this emerges indirectly from his presentation of them. An obvious case is that of Thersites, who is introduced with no pretence of approval:

Thersites alone railed at them, with uncontrolled speech; he knew in his mind many disorderly words, to speak at random and not in decency, to quarrel with the kings. (ii 212–14)

Something of the same contemptuous spirit appears in the account of the beggar Irus:

Then came the public beggar, who went begging through the town of Ithaca; he excelled in his gluttonous belly, to eat and drink without ceasing. He had no strength or force, but in appearance he was very big to look at. (18.1–4)

We naturally assume that such cases illustrate the poet's personal dislike, but we must not rule out the possibility that in them he reflects the views of his noble patrons, who think poorly of such ill-born specimens. It is easy for the poet to agree with them, but at least the characters stand out clearly, even if it is with the clarity of contempt.

A similar objectivity is shown in the presentation of the background against which the actions take place. This must be real and convincing, especially when nature is in question. The Greeks never gave to nature that exclusive attention which later ages have given, nor did they find so much in her. They were not town-dwellers and did not seek a refuge in her, but took her for granted as the setting and the background of their busy lives. In the Homeric poems nature is treated handsomely in the similes and incidentally in the narrative. Twice in the *Odyssey* Homer indulges in what looks like description for description's sake. First there is the cave of Calypso, surrounded by trees of many kinds, mantled with a vine and haunted by sea-birds. Outside it are meadows watered by four streams, and the poet does not conceal his pleasure in it:

There at that time even an immortal would wonder at seeing it and be delighted in his heart. (5.73–4)

The second case is the garden of Alcinous. It is four-square, surrounded by a wall, and rich in fruit-trees and vines. But it has a touch of the miraculous, since the trees and the vines bear fruit all the year round, and one crop follows another in unfailing succession. Each of these scenes serves a purpose. Calypso's cave sets the note for Odysseus' remote exile with a goddess on a lonely island. This is how an immortal nymph lives, but Odysseus does not find it enough and pines to escape and go home. The garden of Alcinous is part of his half-mythical existence. Though he and his Phaeacians are distinguishably human, he lives on the edge of the known world and is entitled to some alleviation of its restrictions.

Such full descriptions are rare and special, but the poems incidentally touch on landscape when it affects the narrative, and give it character and solidity. This is very much the case with the plain of Troy, which presents features that affect the action. Homer appeals to the visual imagination, and the desire for reality creates something clear and clean. This is especially true when something in the landscape has a special significance for the action. More care is taken, and striking results follow. When Achilles fights the river-god Scamander, he calls the fire-god Hephaestus to his succour, and the effects of devastating fire are aptly related:

Elms, willows and tamarisks caught fire; and the lotus and rushes and galingale that grew in plenty about the beautiful banks of the river were burned. Troubled too were the eels and fishes that tumbled in the eddies, this way and that, in the beautiful streams, worn out by the breath of cunning Hephaestus. (xxi 350–5)

This is factual and true to reality. The unusual character of the action needs the precise details which give verisimilitude to it. This manner is not too different from the less dramatic and more unassuming account of Ithaca as Odysseus first sees it after being set ashore in his sleep by the Phaeacians. The harbour itself (13.96–101) is like the modern Vathy, but the description would fit many Greek anchorages, and some of its phrases are used for the harbour of the Laestrygonians (10.87–90). What follows is more individual. At the head of the harbour is an olive-tree and the Cave of the Nymphs, which is carefully described, with its stone formations inside, its water-supply and its two entrances, one on the north for men, one on the south for the gods (13.102–12; 346–8). This serves a real purpose. The treasures of Odysseus must be got out of the way while he deals with the Suitors, and there is much to be said for this unusual hiding-place.

The same selective objectivity can be applied to the works of men. We form our mental picture of Troy almost entirely from its epithets. The palace of Odysseus reveals its plan, never very clearly, when it matters for the story, notably when Penelope comes down from her quarters upstairs or Eumaeus gets out through a small door and a passage concealed in the wall. Nothing is very clear, but in general the palace seems to resemble the so-called Palace of Nestor at Ano Englianos. The small touch that the palace of Circe is made of polished stone increases its strangeness on a lonely island. On the other hand the splendour of the palace of Menelaus at Sparta impels him to explain that all this wealth was gathered on his travels, and so prepares the way for the story of them. The palace of Alcinous has walls of brass, a cornice of blue enamel, golden doors and a silver lintel, and gold and silver dogs on guard, made by Hephaestus (7.86–94). But this, like other things in Phaeacia, is just outside the familiar world and its very wealth prepares the way for the rich gifts which Odysseus is soon to receive from his hosts. Such descriptions were well calculated to suit their place in the story, but their comparative rarity stresses the way in which Homer gives first priority to actions and uses these subsidiary aids to provide background and perspective.

Artefacts, being essential to the action, provide more than decoration and excite professional attention. Though archers are rare in the *Iliad* and Odysseus leaves his great bow at home, the bow of Pandarus, which breaks the truce between the armies, is described at length. It is made from the horns of an ibex which he himself shot; they measure sixteen hands, and have been fitted together, polished and given a golden tip at the end (iv 105–11). The members of the audience would know about archery and appreciate that this was indeed an unusual bow and that its very strangeness fits it for the dramatic purpose of breaking the truce. Even more unusual is the headgear made of boars' teeth on felt which Odysseus wears on night operations. It is described with care (x 261–5), and it seems to be something of an heirloom (x 266–70). In fact it is exactly like a type of Mycenaean helmet of which we have both models and remains, and is by any calculation a remarkable curiosity. We do not know whether Homer had heard of it or actually seen an example, but in either case he knew that was worthy of mention. The poet is a repository of knowledge of the past, and details like this confirm his authority and the worth of his narrative. Perhaps something of the kind is true of the brooch of Odysseus (19.226–31), to which we have no close archaeological parallel, but the scene depicted on it, of a dog throttling a deer, looks like a Mycenaean subject, while the structure of the pins looks much later. The brooch fails as a means to identify the stranger who tells Penelope about it, but adds another clue to the identification of him. When Hera decks herself in her finest finery to allure Zeus and trick him into sleep, it is right that we should be told all about it, and we cannot but note with interest the robe fastened with golden clasps, the girdle with a hundred tassles, the earrings, each with a cluster of four drops, the headdress bright as the sun (14.180–5). All this has a place in Hera's stratagem and needs to be related.

Conversely, sometimes merely utilitarian objects may call for a detailed description if the audience is to envisage exactly what happens. This is the case with the waggon which is loaded with the ransom for Hector and driven by Priam himself. The account (xxiv 266–74) is precise, and special care is given to the way in which the yoke is fastened to the shaft of the waggon. The lead pair are mules, the wheel pair horses, and this may have been an intentional oddity, meant to illustrate how horses trained to chariots in war are less suitable than mules to draw a heavy waggon. We do not know why the fitting of the yoke receives such care. It must have been a fairly familiar action, and the words, being technical, would have no meaning unless they conformed to current usage. The care given may be due to a desire to make the episode absolutely convincing, especially since it is not what is expected in a heroic setting, and its oddity marks it out for special treatment.

Clearly unusual and calling for special care is the raft of Odysseus which he makes with his own hands. It is meant for him alone, and therefore it cannot be large, though it is in fact as wide as a ship of burden (5.249), though not necessarily as long. Odysseus makes it from twenty trees, alder, black poplar and fir, because they will float lightly (5.240), and this suggests that the craft is of no great size, especially as one tree would be needed for the mast, and part of another for the yard. He works with axe, adze and gimlets, and the timbers are well fastened together. It has a sort of deck (5.252), supported by props which protect the voyager from being drenched. It has also a mast and a yard, a rudder or steering oar, and a railing of wicker bulwarks to keep off the spray. Odysseus makes it in three days and even he could not construct a complete ship in that time; it is a raft which he hopes to sail and to steer. In fine weather he can sleep on it on a couch provided with rugs and cloaks by Calypso. This raft not only shows Odysseus' gift for skilled craftsmanship but has a special interest for its unique purpose, which is to carry a crew of one for a voyage of seventeen days. The careful account is worthy of the important occasion when Odysseus, after eight years with Calypso prepares to leave and travel alone over the unknown sea. He works with knowledge and precision, and it is not his technical fault that the raft fails to finish its journey.

Quite different from these solid, workaday descriptions is one notable long passage in which Homer gives a full account of the shield which Hephaestus makes for Achilles to take the place of that seized by Hector from the body of Patroclus (xviii 478–608). The shield is not something that the poet himself has seen. It is too elaborate, too costly, too accomplished, but we may speculate from what sources he invented it. Its technique of gold, silver, tin and blue enamel is not unlike that of the dagger-blades from the shaft-tombs at Mycenae. Some object, not necessarily on this enormous scale, may have survived into Homer's time and excited his wonder. Equally, even if all such objects had disappeared in the intervening centuries, they may have left memories in formulaic song. In the passage of years the accounts might lose something of accuracy, and of course each new bard could, if he wished, make his own improvements. The shield, with its concentric scenes of nature and human life, could only be a decorative object, quite unfit for use in battle, but that need not trouble Homer who profits from the loss of Achilles' armour to embark on a splendid piece of descriptive poetry. In battle the splendour of the new armour does not matter and is hardly mentioned. For the moment it is a rich flight of imagination and we take it as it comes. The shield is the handiwork of a god, suited to the half-divine hero Achilles, and in the broad range of the subjects depicted on it is a microcosm of life as Homer knew it. It gives him a chance to extend his scope beyond the battlefield and the doings of heroes into other less exalted but not less attractive fields. It is Homer's ideal work of art, what he thinks metal-work could be in the hands of a god, and it is noteworthy that six times he uses adjectives which convey much the same note of admiration, 'beautiful', 'lovely' and 'awaking desires'. These are applied to the scenes made by Hephaestus, not to any possible originals they may have copied in nature or human society. The shield is what art ought to be—a representation of things in a beautiful way. It gives delight, and is to this degree comparable to heroic song. Nor is it reckless to imagine that in conceiving this supreme work of art Homer tried to do for visual art what he himself did for words. Both arts transform reality, and in this their beauty lies.

The strength of the poetical tradition can be seen in the knowledge which the *Iliad* reveals of Troy and the Trojan plain. We have seen how apt the epithets for these are, but there is more to be considered than epithets. The *Iliad* has a good general grasp of Troy in its geographical setting, and from the top of Hisarlik we can identify most of the sites which Homer mentions. The Achaean camp could be set to the north, where the coast takes a sharp turn eastwards, and the battlefield is between this and the city. At some distance to the west are the twin peaks of Samothrace, from which Poseidon watches the battle (xiii 12–14). To the east, and much closer, is Mount Ida, whence Zeus in his turn watches the battle (viii 47 ff.), and from which wood is brought to make a pyre for Patroclus (xxiii 117 ff.). Nearer home, to the east of Achaean camp and still identifiable, in the village of Keren Koi, is the high ground Callicolone, where the gods who favour Troy gather (xx 151). On the plain itself is a slight elevation, which suits the place where the Trojans gather before an attack (xi 56; xx 3).

These small touches suggest some knowledge of the terrain, and this knowledge is at times used with dramatic effect. The large view from the top of Hisarlik confirms the ease with which Helen points out the Achaean leaders from the walls (iii 161 ff.). When Achilles fights the river-god Scamander and Hephaestus comes to his rescue and burns all the vegetation.

Burned were the elms and the willows and the tamarisks, and burned was the clover and the rushes and the galingale. (xxi 350–1)

This is the vegetation which still flourishes on Trojan river-banks. When Achilles pursues Hector three times round Troy, we might expect it to be a heroic prodigy, but in fact the distance is not great, nor the terrain very difficult. When Priam goes out at night to visit Achilles in the Achaean camp, he can travel easily in a wagon, for almost the whole journey is over level ground. When Achilles drags Hector's body behind this chariot round Troy, Andromache comes out of her house on to the walls by a tower and sees what is happening (xxii 460 ff.). These are but small points, but in them the physical setting adds something to the story. Once or twice it does so more unexpectedly. When

Patroclus attempts to scale the walls of Troy, he tries three times and three times he fails:

'Three times Patroclus moved on to the angle of the lofty wall, and three times Apollo drove him away by force'. (xvi 702–3)

Now it happens that the lower part of the walls of Troy are at an angle which makes it not too difficult to climb them, but at the top of this were perpendicular battlements. Patroclus reaches the angle (literally 'elbow'), where these meet, and is pushed down. A batter of this kind is rare, and this looks like a genuine reminiscence. Again, Andromache tells Hector:

'Station the host by the wild fig-tree, where the city is most easily approached and the wall may be scaled'. (vi 433–4)

It happens that the excavations have revealed a weak spot in the western fortifications, and of this the passage may contain some echo.

Not everything in the Homeric scene of Troy can be substantiated, and one or two problems remain unsolved. First, the two rivers Scamander and Simois may be identified with the modern Mendere and In-tepe Asmak, but in the flat plain these rivers often change their courses and we have no assurance that their present position is what was known to Homer. On the whole his picture is clear. The two rivers flow, very roughly parallel, across the plain to the sea. But two points are difficult. First, it looks as if the battle swayed between the rivers without obstacle, and yet at one point we heard that the rivers join their streams (v 774). It does not much matter, but it may come from a time when the rivers had different courses, and the battle would not flow easily between them. Secondly, there are three places where there is a ford over Scamander (xiv 432; xxi 1 ff.; xxiv 349, 692). We might expect the ford to be a place to cross the river, but this seems to be used for watering horses and then passed on the flank—not impossible but curious. A similar difficulty arises with the hot and cold springs which Hector and Achilles pass in their race (xxii 147–56). The description is exact and convincing and looks like a real memory

37, 38. *Excavations of the palace of Nestor at Pylos (Ano Englianos)*
showing ABOVE *the great hearth in the throne room and* BELOW *a bathroom*
with bath. Homer describes Nestor's palace in the Odyssey, *and may have*
created Odysseus' own palace on Ithaca in its image (see p. 145)

39. *The real Ithaca is rocky, but not low-lying. Aetos* ABOVE, *in this nineteenth-century engraving, is where Schliemann thought Odysseus' palace was sited. A more likely site is in the north, near Polis Bay*

but though the Troad offers some natural hot springs, no springs like these have been discovered. Time may have changed them, or perhaps legend, knowing something not very accurately, has built up a picture. Yet neither with the springs nor with the rivers can we say that the *Iliad* is wrong. Such divagations as it presents from the present geography can be explained by the changes brought by time.

If we allow that much of the knowledge of Troy, such as that displayed by the epithets, is of ancient origin, it is always possible that the living poet has made his own contributions and may even have visited the site of Troy, which was beginning to revive in the eighth century with Greek colonists. For this there are certain not final, but at least favourable, arguments. First, the account of the landscape is remarkably consistent and creates no difficulties. A poet working only with traditional material might well make blunders, and his failure to do so suggests that he knows something of the subject. Secondly, the country and the city are used with great dramatic effect, whether in the ebb and flow of battle or the nocturnal journey of Priam or the appearance of characters on the city walls. Such use would come more readily with actual knowledge.

Ithaca, which is the scene for much of the *Odyssey*, presents a different case. Historically this small, rocky, and barren island had one great advantage. It stood off the western end of the Gulf of Corinth and commanded the sea-ways to and from the west. This may account for its place in legend. Nor need we doubt that Homer's Ithaca is in some sense the modern Thiaki or Ithaki, which has kept the name through the centuries. What we may doubt is how much the poet knew of it. Some at least of his story fits into the modern island. Odysseus is landed in the harbour of Phorcys, which corresponds to Vathy. His palace is some way from this and may be placed on the west of the island at Polis. The steading of Eumaeus fits the southern part of the island and the remote dwelling of Laertes the northern. The adjective 'under Neius' (3.81) agrees with Mount Anoi. There is a recognizable fountain of Arethusa (13.408), and a small harbour of St Andrea on the south coast, where Telemachus can land on his return from Pylos (15.497). Not quite so neat but still possible, if we allow for poetical transformation, is a cave near but not very near to Vathy, which will serve as the cave of the Nymphs (13.347 ff.), though it is not immediately by the harbour. Perhaps the island of Dhascalio, in the strait between Ithaca and Cefalonia, will do for the island of Asteris, behind which the Suitors lie in ambush (4.844–7). It may not matter that the modern island is much too small, since it may have been reduced by earthquakes. So far the Homeric Ithaca betrays some local knowledge, which got into the tradition, despite the remoteness of Ithaca from Ionia. We might even think that these details come from a time before the migrations eastward. But this is not the whole story. There are places where the *Odyssey* speaks of Ithaca in a way which does not suit the present island, still less the semi-island of Leucas, with which it has sometimes been identified. The chief of these is the account given by Odysseus himself to Alcinous:

'Itself it is low-lying, and lies, furthest out, in the sea towards the gloom, and the other islands are separate towards the east and the sun.'
(9.25–6)

This contains three false statements. Ithaca is not low-lying, and we have no right to say that the word means 'near the shore', which anyhow it is not. It is not furthest out, even if we assume that the coast was thought to run east to west, which of course it does not. So far from the other islands being to the east and the sun, they are to the south, west and north. It looks as if while the tradition was still forming and new features were added, somebody who knew almost nothing about Ithaca added these lines to make it more convincing.

What counts most in the Homeric poems is action. It awakes the responses through which we judge the poetry. To the range of these responses there is almost no limit. There is almost no human reaction which Homer did not translate into a concrete poetical form. The one of which he is a little sparing is laughter. This is applied abundantly to the gods, who laugh at each other and whose merriment is presumably shared by the poet's audience, especially in such full-scale episodes as the Deception of Zeus or the song of Demodocus on the love of Ares and Aphrodite. Among men this is much rarer. It is true that there is gentle fun in the exchange of armour between Glaucus and Diomedes (vi 235–6), where the generous impulse of Glaucus makes him give away his golden armour in exchange for the bronze armour of Diomedes, which is worth only a ninth of it. There are too outbursts of bitter laughter, as when the Achaeans laugh at the blow which Odysseus gives to Thersites with his sceptre (ii 270) or the frenzied laughter of the Suitors which Athene sends to them (20.346). But this is not humour, but derision and, as such, well fitted to the heroic temper in its wilder or angrier moods.

With this partial exception there is almost no human emotion which Homer does not present or which he does not arouse. His effect is the more powerful because it is direct, immediate and single. He may be compared first with other practitioners of oral heroic song, and we mark the enormous difference of range between him and not merely the author of the *Song of Roland* and the poets of the *Elder Edda* but the authors of *Gilgamesh* and *Beowulf*, to say nothing of Mongol or Tatar poets still or recently at work. These other poets have indeed moments of concentrated force and assertive power, but so has Homer; what they have not got in his wonderful range which seems to cover all human experience that is worth covering. Heroic poets are not expected to do this; their job is rather to catch certain high moments and concentrate on them. Homer has an effortless grasp of most elementary human states, and moves easily from one to another. Conversely, he may be compared, in quite a different respect, with those poets, writers of literary epic, who sought to imitate and rival and improve him. Of these Virgil is first and foremost. Though he knew that he could never really rival Homer in his own field, he still tried to do something comparable, and attained at least a noble scope and dignity. He is hampered by his own contorted, conflicting, uncertain emotions and by his insecurity of belief and outlook. By trying to believe more than he did he succeeded in believing less, and his vision of imperial Rome is much vaguer than Homer's vivid sense of heroic manhood. Homer would not have maintained his wonderful directness of approach if he had not sung to a listening audience and felt himself bound to make everything beautifully clear to it. Conversely, in exploiting a far wider range of themes than other heroic poets he may have been helped by the wealth and antiquity of the Greek poetical tradition which accumulated stories over a long period, and reflected a generous taste for life because it was almost the only fine art that flourished in the dark ages after the collapse of the Mycenaean civilization. A poet could take advantage of this and learn from it, but he would not have gained much if he had not possessed to a very high degree the imaginative insight and the creative understanding which turn human emotions into poetry.

In depicting the emotions at work Homer makes his audience share them and enter into the spirit of his characters. This happens so effortlessly that we hardly notice it, but the ease is largely due to Homer's concentration on a single mood and his subjection of everything to this. Thus the quarrel between Agamemnon and Achilles in Book i is a study in anger on both sides. Each hero is dominated by it because he thinks that he has been wounded in his honour, Agamemnon by having to give up Chryseis, Achilles by having Briseis taken from him. Anger flares through the book and takes vivid forms, from rabid abuse to thoughts of violence which come very near to action. In the exchange of insults the two heroes are well matched. We may not for the moment ask who has right on his side, and it is not till later that we see the case of Achilles. This is the authentic Homeric technique. The simple, powerful emotions promote swift and overwhelming action. The high temper displayed by the two heroes is self-destructive and leads to untold harm, but it can take other, less deadly forms, and in any case it is essential to the action on the battlefield, to the impetus which carries Hector or Patroclus, Diomedes or Sarpedon, on his unrelenting course. It sets the tone for the fiercest events, and everything follows naturally.

Just as in his construction of narrative Homer follows the rule of 'one thing at a time', so this enforces on him a simplification and indeed a simplicity of poetical effect. Every episode has on the whole a single character, but once it is finished we may expect something quite different. Once his direction is set, he goes irresistibly ahead. So when Iris tells Achilles to appear at the trench and dismay the Trojans, she does it after scenes of lamentation and grief, but at this point Homer takes a new direction and the whole passage (xviii 202–31) is an astonishing display of what the mere appearance of Achilles can do. A fierce, heroic splendour shines in every line, and it is right and proper that at the sight twelve Trojan charioteers die of shock. So too, when Odysseus strings the bow, we are held in tense expectation, but the whole situation moves forward with increasing excitement as he first shoots an arrow down the line of the axes and then leaps upon the platform, throws off his rags, and announces his new task of vengeance. The tone is suddenly changed and then maintained for the new actions.

This concentration is applied to quite small matters, and does much to integrate them into the main poem. For instance in Book i the angry quarrel between Agamemnon and Achilles is interrupted by a description of the voyage in which Odysseus brings back Chryseis to her father (i 430–87). It tells the successive stages of the voyage, the landing, the welcome, the feast, and the departure. Each is factual and precise and brief, and the whole episode breaks for a few moments the violence of the quarrels behind it. It is quite wrong to think it an interpolation; it fulfils a need, and it does so by keeping its own quiet tone without a mistake. Rather more exciting but equally well maintained is the small episode in which Odysseus, drawing unknown near to the hut of Eumaeus, is attacked by the dogs and fortunately rescued by the swineherd. It is a sudden moment of excitement, admirably sustained, entirely true to Greek life, and an excellent introduction to Eumaeus. The different elements are fused into a single whole, which has a character different both from what precedes and from what succeeds it.

The direct movement of narrative is enriched by Homer's eye

for the illuminating detail, the small touch which throws a vivid
light on what happens. Thersites, for instance, makes only one
appearance in the *Iliad*, but though it is short it is important
because he embodies unheroic, even anti-heroic qualities, and
these are reflected in his appearance:

He was the ugliest man who came to Troy. He was bandy-legged and
lame in one foot. His shoulders were bent and met over his chest. Above,
he had an egg-shaped head, and on it sprouted some scanty hairs.
(ii 216–19)

Such an appearance fits Thersites' character and behaviour and
marks him out for contempt. Less obviously brutal but no less
telling is the introduction of Dolon:

He had much gold and much bronze. He was ugly to look at but fast
on his feet, and he was an only son, with five sisters. (x 315–17)

This is nicely damaging and makes it easier to endure Dolon's
death which soon follows. Such touches are unexpected and
sometimes bizarre, but they are delightfully apt. A small but
delightful touch comes from Menelaus when he tells how Helen
walked round the Wooden Horse and addressed the Achaean
leaders, imitating the voices of their wives (4.279). We can believe
it of her, but it is told so simply that it takes a moment to see how
illuminating it is. So too when a very unusual situation is in
question, Homer makes sense of it by some deft stroke of insight.
When Menelaus lies in wait for the sea-god Proteus, he and his
companions hide by wrapping themselves in newly-flayed seal-
skins:

'There would our lying-in-wait have been most horrible, for the deadly
stink of the sea-bred seals wore us down terribly; for who would lie
down to rest by a creature of the sea?' (4.441–3)

Fortunately they are saved by the goddess putting ambrosia under
their nostrils—but the point has been made, and illustrates the
unusual nature of the adventure.

Such small touches may give a powerful reinforcement to some
general effect which is intended. When Hector, takes advantage

of a lull in the battle to go into Troy, he finds his wife Andromache on the walls. They exchange touching and beautiful words about the dark prospects that face them, and then Hector turns to his small child Astyanax:

After speaking, Hector reached out his arms for his child; but the child shrank back crying to the bosom of his deep-girdled nurse, frightened helmet. His dear father and his lady mother laughed. Then shining hair plume, which he marked as it nodded terrible from the crest of the helmet. His dear father and his lady mother laughed. Then shining Hector took the helmet from his head, and set it, all glittering, on the ground. (vi 466–73)

This changes the tone, which is beginning to reach a tragic temper, and introduces the warmth of a young family, but the one rises out of the other, since the child is the token of the love of Hector and Andromache The common, human touch adds to the grandeur and nobility of the occasion. So too when Achilles has tied the dead Hector to his chariot and is already dragging him round Troy, Andromache does not yet know what is happening. She is busy with her embroidery, and then she gives orders to her slaves to heat the water for Hector's bath when he comes back from battle (xxii 440–4). She then hears the sound of wailing, rushes out and sees the worst. The small domestic touches mark the gap between the life of a woman and the life of a man, and their juxtaposition shows how closely interwoven they are. At a less tragic level but deeply touching is the dog Argos, who recognizes Odysseus after twenty years and then dies (17.326–7). He is the true and faithful servant who knows his master without any marks or signs, and suffers for his loyalty as he lies cast on the midden, neglected and full of ticks. These are an indication of his loyalty, and death is the right end at the right time.

In these cases, and in many others like them, a detail adds something highly individual and yet illuminating, and such details are more effective when they strengthen some display of emotion or affection. They are as necessary to the heroic outlook as any kind of prowess, for they provide the hero with a solid background and bind his friends to him. The *Iliad*, like other heroic poems, has its examples of heroic friendship, not only in Achilles and Patroclus but on the Trojan side in Sarpedon and Glaucus. These friendships find their chief outlet in war, where each friend helps the other, and if either is in trouble he calls for the other's help. So Sarpedon reminds Glaucus that they receive great honours in their own homeland, which they do not deserve if they fail to rise to the present challenge; so let them take the risk and advance to battle (xii 310–28). Later, when Sarpedon has been mortally wounded by Patroclus, he calls on his friend to look after his body and his armour after his death (xvi 492–501), and this Glaucus, with the help of the gods, does.

The affection between Achilles and Patroclus is more powerful and more tragic, since Achilles feels that he failed to save Patroclus (xviii 98–100). So long as Patroclus is alive Achilles treats him as an equal and shares his troubles with him. When Patroclus is deeply distressed by the disasters of the Achaeans, Achilles mocks him gently and compares him to a child running to its mother (xvi 7–11), but when he knows what the trouble is, he treats it seriously and not only lets Patroclus go to battle but lends him his own armour. The strength of his love for Patroclus is revealed when the latter is killed, and takes almost extravagant forms (xviii 23 ff.), so that Antilochus is afraid that Achilles will cut his throat from grief. Because Patroclus has been killed by Hector, Achilles is obsessed by a desire to kill Hector in return (xviii 114), but even this is not enough for him, and when he has killed Hector, his troubles are not finished.

These male affections are stronger and more demanding than affections between men and women. Since the woman is dependent on the man, she finds her fulfilment in him. Andromache's whole life is centred on Hector and their small child. Indeed they can hardly be otherwise; for her whole family has been killed by Achilles (vi 421–4), and her husband takes their place:

'Hector, you are my father and my lady mother and my brother, and you are my sturdy husband.' (vi 429–30)

In her love for him she foresees his death and knows that it means the end for herself and her child. Yet in this there is nothing mawkish. Andromache lives entirely for her duties as a wife and a mother, but she has her woman's honour which lies in her husband's prowess. She is still a very young woman, and her pathos is enhanced by it, but she is not pathetic in any cheap or commonplace way. She knows what the dangers are and she is ready to face them.

In this matter there is a great difference between Achilles and Hector. Even in battle it is noteworthy that while one of Hector's gifts is for rallying and inspiring his fellows, Achilles needs no support and fights alone. This reflects the great difference between their personal lives. Patroclus is deeply attached to Achilles, but hardly says so, and complains that he is not the son of Peleus and Thetis but of the sea and the rocks (xvi 33–5). Patroclus may even be said to die for Achilles in so far as his career in battle is caused by his shame at Achilles' abstention from it. But the ties between them are quite different from the steady, quiet devotion which bind Andromache and Hector. Nor is Thetis dependent on Achilles in any respect. She is deeply involved in his life, and feels his sorrows all the more because he is doomed to die young (i 415–18). This is about all the affection which Achilles inspires, and the contrast is complete with Hector, who is the mainstay not only of Andromache but of Priam, who sees in his death the end of Troy (xxii 410–11), of Hecuba, who loves him more than all her other children (xxiv 748), and of Helen, who is deeply conscious of his kindness to her (xxiv 761–75). In the scarcity of his human ties Achilles stands out more emphatically as a hero, while Hector is a little too human to be a hero of the highest class. Yet both are presented through the affections that they arouse in others or feel for them. It is not their only claim, but it is a background against which their other qualities show their worth. It is right that they should be pitted against each other, and each gains something by it.

In the study of Homeric affections Odysseus and Penelope have a special place. When we are introduced to them, they have been severed for twenty years, and after all this time Penelope cherishes his memory and breaks constantly into tears at the thought of him. She is convinced that he is dead, but such is her love for him that she clings to hope and trusts that every rumour of his survival may be true. She does not speak explicitly of her love for him. That is taken for granted, and yet, when he is at last restored to her, her inbred suspicion is strong and she hesitates before she accepts him. This is true to human nature, and after all he has been away for a very long time. On his side Odysseus is almost equally undemonstrative, but he reveals his true feelings to Calypso when, to no purpose, she hopes that he will stay with her, and he answers:

'Lady goddess, be not angry with me in this way; I too know very well that wise Penelope is inferior to you in looks and figure for the eyes to see; for she is a mortal woman, and you are immortal and free from old age. But even so I wish and hope all my days to go home and see the day of my return.' (5.215–20)

When at the end of a long story husband and wife are alone together they pick up an old intimacy and Penelope cannot take her arms off her husband (23.240). This decorous, lasting affection does not touch us very deeply, and we cannot but compare it with the love which Odysseus' mother, Anticlea, feels for him, and which we hear of when he calls up her ghost at the end of the world. He asks her what brought her death, and she answers:

'The far-seeing shooter of arrows did not come upon me in my chambers or kill me with her gentle shafts, nor did any sickness attack me, such as most often takes away life from the limbs with hideous wasting. But it was longing for you and for your ways, glorious Odysseus, and for your gentleness of heart, that took away life from my limbs.' (11.197–203)

This is the most direct and most powerful outburst of affection in Homer, and it illustrates how his concentration on a single mood gives a uniquely dramatic power.

When Homer has exploited a single mood or tone, he changes to another, and this too is done simply but conclusively. The most complex case is in Book ix when an embassy comes to Achilles to make amends for Agamemnon and to ask him to relent, but he refuses and they go away unsuccessful. Inside this main plan of failure Homer marks three stages and each makes a dramatic surprise. At 357 ff. Achilles announces that he will sail away on the morrow; at 618 ff. that he will sail away in the morning; at 650–3 that he will join battle when Hector reaches the ships of the Myrmidons. Though for the moment these amount to a refusal, in the long run they mark stages towards the still distant moment when Achilles will return to battle. The change is deftly and delicately presented, and each section has its own character. So too in the exploits of Patroclus there is a marked variation of tone and effect. In the first stage he carries all before him (xvi 278–675). Then Apollo opposes him, and the mood changes to uncertainty, doubt, and alarm, until finally Patroclus is wounded and disarmed and killed (xvi 676–861). The two phases are quite distinct; each has its own marked character, the first working through the thrills of a victorious progress, the second through a sense of forthcoming failure and defeat.

The emotions which Homer shows at work are those of living beings, human or divine or animal. In the last class are the horse of Achilles and the dog of Odysseus, both deeply concerned with their masters and each showing it in his own way, the horse by speaking in a human voice, the dog by wagging its tail and dying. The gods are close to us because they are like human beings. They are vastly more powerful and do what men cannot possibly do, but this somehow enhances their likeness and makes us treat them as we would men who are not doomed to die. They have distinct personalities and move in their own right. Each of the three goddesses, Athene, Hera and Aphrodite, is moved by proper pride, as heroes are, and pursues her enemies without qualm. But the gods are brought closer to men in other, more interesting ways. First, they have their human children. Aphrodite is the mother of Aeneas, and protects him in battle; Zeus is the father of Sarpedon and would protect him if it were possible. Though they themselves cannot really be hurt, the gods can be wounded in their affections when their children suffer. Secondly, the gods have their human attachment. We have seen how strong is Athene's for Odysseus, but in a different way Aphrodite's care for Paris is hardly less strong, though less friendly and intimate. Because he gave her the prize of beauty, she gives him Helen, and both saves him from death in the duel with Menelaus and consoles him by forcing Helen to do what he wishes. The affections of the gods do not touch us very deeply but make the gods more likeable. It is the other side of their hatreds, of the injured pride which compels them to maintain unceasing hostility to those who have in some sense dishonoured them. That is why Athene and Hera fight on the other side to Aphrodite, why Poseidon harries Odysseus for blinding Polyphemus and hates Troy because he was cheated by Laomedon (xxi 443 ff.).

By giving human traits to his gods and his animals Homer unifies his approach to his complex subject, and this attitude helps to explain his intention in composition. It is clear on all sides that he does not wish to instruct. His comments on the action are hardly ever his own, but are made by the characters on each other. Even if the Trojan War is due to the shamelessness of Paris in preferring Aphrodite to Hera and Athene (xxiv 30), the poet does not actually condemn Paris; he merely reports why the gods acted as they did, and assumes that Paris was, as he is elsewhere, mad about women (iii 39; xiii 769). Nor elsewhere does he condemn any action by one of his characters, or even praise one. Nor is it clear that he tells his tale to instil ideals of manhood and present models of it for imitation. He certainly holds these ideals and they give shape to his narrative, but he does not underline them or drive them home. In later times Homer was regarded as a teacher of the young, well versed in the right kinds of behaviour and able to give vivid instances of it, but this was simply a means to justify the study of him in schools. When Plato attacks him for his low view of the gods or his over-indulgence in the emotions, it was because these were accepted as norms of behaviour. But there is no reason to think that Homer himself created types of manhood for imitation or even as warnings. His personalities derive their being from his passionate interest in them, and this itself may well have been fostered by a tradition which rejoiced in the glorious doings of men. This is the central spring of his power and if incidentally he inspires or instructs, it is because he believes so strongly in the reality and worth of certain human qualities. No doubt he composes poetry because he must, and that is explanation enough.

In his poetry Homer wishes to give delight. This is the intention which he ascribes to his imaginary bards. Telemachus explains to Penelope that Phemius gives pleasure as his spirit moves him (1.347), and Alcinous speaks of Demodocus in similar words (8.45). Both ascribe this power to a god and so exalt it. When Homer invents a father for Phemius he calls him Terpiades (22.330), where the root *terp-* is that of the word 'delight'. This is a kind of enchantment. Penelope uses the word 'enchantments' of songs in general (1.337), and when Odysseus tells his own story, the audience is held 'by a spell' (11.334; 13.2). Since the bard is inspired by a god, it is right that his song should have a magical power of holding his hearers. This view presupposes a high level of style and outlook. Homer aims not at mere enjoyment, but at enjoyment of a lofty kind which comes from the gods and holds the attention of men. This view of poetry is by no means unique, but seems to be held quite often in circles where heroic song is honoured. The bards are so sure of the worth of their material and of their own ability to handle it that they can afford to present it without didactic or moralistic additions. It is later that the poet becomes a teacher, as he certainly did in Greece. Homer's impact is different, and all the stronger because he is concerned primarily with the vivid presentation of human beings. Moreover, since he presents them in action, he makes them living entities without any of the distortion introduced by abstraction and instruction.

Homer has his own view of the place of song in the world. This he states both in the *Iliad* and in the *Odyssey*, and though the words vary a little, and suggest that they are not strictly formulaic, the main substance is the same. In the *Iliad* Helen tells Hector that she and Paris are the cause of the troubles of Troy:

'Upon us Zeus set an evil doom, that afterwards we may be sung of by men to come.' (vi 357–8)

In the *Odyssey*, before Odysseus begins his long story, Alcinous, noticing his distress, on hearing a tale of Troy, says of this doom:

'The gods fashioned it, and they wove destruction for men that they might be a song for those in the future.' (8.579–80)

This is a clear and emphatic view, and not what we should expect to find in Homer or what in fact we find in other heroic poetry. It asserts the supremacy of art over human fortunes and justifies them because of the pleasure which songs about them will give. Whatever the social position or authority of the poet was, he had no doubt of the importance of his art, and he asserts this confidently through two important witnesses, Helen and Alcinous. Even though we argue that this belief is relevant to Helen's own case and helps her to endure her troubles, Alcinous is above the battle and offers consolation to the much-enduring Odysseus. No doubt Homer's own patrons were comforted by the thought that their doings would be remembered in song; Homer himself went further and saw in song a consolation and an explanation of the ills and sufferings of mankind. It commemorates them and transcends them, and raises them to an unperishing order of being.

CHAPTER NINE

The Creative Outlook

HOMER told of a heroic age, which he regarded as much superior to his own. Not being a historian, he does not place it in any datable past, and though we can find a historical foundation for it, Homer's picture is compounded of so many different elements that it corresponds to nothing real. For him, as for us, its reality comes from the poetical imagination which has made it. In this he has profited enormously from the work of others and is only one poet among many. We cannot help asking how he gave strength and solidity to this mythical past. On the one hand he gained much from tradition which told of certain aspects of the past and through its vivid outline of them, whether in personalities or in material circumstances, or in dramatic events, provided a basis for poetry. On the other hand this skeleton did not take on flesh and blood until Homer had clothed it with infinite observations of his own time, of men and women and animals, of a living scene which he saw every day, and which enabled him to view the past as vividly as the present. In this process Homer's own genius is continually at work. It gives new life and fullness to the outlines offered by tradition, and it shows his own tastes and inclinations as he shapes the present to fuse with the past. In this process the nature of the tradition and the character of Homer's own world compete for his creative enterprise.

In this matter Homer's audience plays an essential part. If we may judge by Phemius and Demodocus and assume that they represent his own condition, then his patrons were princes and chieftains, and other people of less social importance were excluded from his performance. In this there is nothing strange. These

privileged few are after all the people who wish to hear about
heroes because they claim to be descended from them and see
themselves as displaying some of their virtues. If this is correct
Homer's audiences were probably like those of the *Elder Edda* in
the halls of Norse chieftains or of *Gilgamesh*, whose text survives
in the royal library of Assurbanipal. It is clear that the Homeric
poems were not meant for a proletarian audience which maintained
its own relaxations when an upper class had found something else
to its taste. There is no sign that poetry had sunk in the social
scale or been displaced as the centre of high relaxation. On the
other hand it is possible that the audience was not confined to
princes and nobles, that the performance was in some sense open
and the poems available to a wide range of human beings. If so,
the circumstances in which Phemius and Demodocus sing will
have been extended and enlarged, and this may have had some
influence on the contents of the songs.

Yet it is indubitable that the Homeric poems display a strong
aristocratic bias; they tell of great men of the past for great men of
the present. Here, as elsewhere, heroic poetry is primarily a
perquisite of princes and nobles. They set its tone and impose their
tastes and requirements on it. Even if performances are not
confined to them but are on certain occasions open to all and
sundry, the aristocratic temper remains and is obvious in the
treatment of those characters who are not in a high position.
Eumaeus, the swineherd of Odysseus, is a king's son, who was
trapped into slavery in childhood; the other humble employees
are judged by their loyalty to the ruling house, and if they fail in
it, come to hideous ends. The rank and file in the *Iliad* have a part
in the fighting, but we are told very little indeed about it. Both
poems have an aristocratic bias, such as does not exist in the works
of Hesiod, which may not be very much later in date and present
from inside the anxious world of the struggling farmer, who makes
no attempt to observe heroic standards. The difference between
Homer and Hesiod can be seen from a small point. Hesiod tells
how certain men devour bribes, and 'give judgments by crooked
decisions' (*Works and Days* 221). This refers to the local magis-

trates, who give judgments not from written laws but from their hereditary information. Homer is acquainted with these ideas and presents them in a long and striking simile, which tells how in autumn violent rains and storms vex the earth:

When Zeus is furiously angry with men, who despite him in the market-place give judgments by crooked decisions, and drive out justice giving no thought to the wrath of the gods. (xvi 386–8).

Each poet uses the same formula for giving crooked decisions, and clearly the theme had a place in tradition. But whereas Hesiod suggests that the kings take bribes and are most concerned in justice and injustice, Homer does not mention them in this context, though it is clear that his sceptre-holding kings are in fact also judges (ii 86). In this simile Homer might be thought to suggest that kings can be unjust and provoke the wrath of Zeus in storms, but in fact he just avoids this. He uses the established formula, and refers not to 'kings' but to 'men'.

It certainly looks as if heroic poetry were in the first place intended for princes and nobles, and their tastes and requirements shaped its choice and treatment of subjects, its general outlook, and its emphasis on birth and breeding. These conditions are to be found in it at every point, but it does not follow that all poets working in the tradition were not interested in men and women outside the heroic world of legend. No doubt in shaping his main characters Homer had his own notion of what a hero should be, and strengthened his creation with his own insight and observation. This is certainly true of his more vivid or more complex creations. It is conceivable that he formed his Achilles and his Odysseus from his own interpretation of legend without deriving much from living men around him, but this can hardly have been the case with characters less obviously heroic, especially women. Nausicaa is a wonderful creation, entirely natural and delightful and dignified, and she is as far as possible from the ruthlessly heroic women whom we know from the *Elder Edda*. Homer in fact presents no such women. Perhaps they existed in Greek poetry when it told of the Amazon Penthesilea, whom Achilles kills, but there is no sign that Homer cares for them. His Helen is surely his own version of what she ought to be, not something imposed on him by tradition. Even Circe, whose actions can be highly sinister, does not reveal her hawk-like qualities once Odysseus has mastered her, and Calypso, lonely and neglected, shows no disagreeable traits such as we expect in a witch. It is more than probable that even when Homer derived the outline of a character from tradition, he added flesh and blood to it, and that when tradition was not very informative he created freely from his knowledge of the living world.

That he was deeply concerned with the living world is clear from his similes and in a smaller degree from the Shield of Achilles. Here we see the living world which engaged his affectionate attention, and though it is far removed from the heroic world of his story, it too is full of struggle and danger. Life for Homer's contemporaries can seldom have been secure; for many it was bleak and poverty-stricken; for all it was threatened at many points alike by nature and by man. War was a common feature of it, and appears on the Shield when a city at war is contrasted with a city at peace (xviii 509–40). So too a closely associated pair of similes tell first of a city beleaguered by enemies and sending up fire-signals for help (xviii 207–14), then of a trumpet sounding to warn citizens against an enemy attack (xviii 219–20). The trumpet seems not to have had a place in the poetical tradition, and the mention of it comes from the contemporary world. What war means to ordinary people can be seen from the full and touching account of a woman weeping over the body of her slain husband, while the victors prod her with spears to take her into bondage (8.523–30).

This sense of struggle goes much deeper. The most fearful force against which men have to struggle is nature, whether in the sea or in the form of wild animals. Homer knows all about the sea, and his similes stress its uncertainties and risks, whether when a wave breaks over the gunwale (xv 381–3), or a violent wind roars into the sail and the sailors are near death (xv 624–8), or when a ship is wrecked at sea and only some of the crew survive by swimming to land (23.233–8). This is the historical background to the shipwreck and other nautical adventures of Odysseus, and though the tradition may have preserved items of interest, Homer knew more from his own time. The perils of the sea are balanced by the perils of the land, notably from wild beasts which attack and destroy the flocks and herds which are the main source of livelihood. The chief enemy is the lion, and though it had disappeared from almost all the Greek mainland by the fifth century, there is no reason to think that it did not thrive on the coastlands of Asia Minor when Homer composed his poems. There is no doubt that he knew of lions and their victories and defeats. He tells from every angle of man's fight to protect his flocks from lions. A lion gains courage when he finds himself among sheep (v 136–42); two lions roam the hills at ease and snatch oxen until men kill them (v 554–8); a lion has got into a steading and retreats very unwillingly despite the javelins and torches thrown at him (xi 546–55); in his hunger he breaks into a farm but finds men on guard and has either to run away or be wounded (xii 299–306); men hunting deer or wild goat suddenly come across a lion, who frightens them away (xv 271–6); suddenly appearing among cattle, a lion takes what he wants while he terrifies the rest (xv 630–6); a hungry lion, beaten by wind and rain, is not afraid of going into a solid steading (6.130–4); he comes up against a sturdy defence of dogs and hunters, but he is not afraid of it, and his courage brings his death (xii 41–8). Wild boars are hardly less dangerous and are equated with lions for strength and violence. Pastoral life called for continual vigilance and active defence, and was in its way a counterpart to life on the battlefield. Even on the shield, where the scenes are highly selective and significant, there is one where lions attack a bull, and the shepherds can do nothing since their dogs do nothing to attack the lions (xviii 574–86).

This sense of continual struggle and danger enhances Homer's appreciation of the common activities of his kind. Behind these active defences life goes on with its small pleasures and its daily activities. Even this has its moments of violence, as when two women slang each other in the street (xx 252–5) or two men dispute a boundary (xii 421–3). It has too its moments of grief, as when a father laments his son as he cremates his bones (xxiii 222–3), or its moments of relief, as when a father unexpectedly recovers from sickness (5.394–7). Homer knows the pathos of the poor, as of the woman who works at wool that 'she may win a shameful wage for her children' (xii 433–5). There is a real touch of tenderness in the mother who wards off a fly from her child as he sleeps (iv 130–1), or when a woman in childbirth feels 'a sharp stabbing weapon' (xi 269–71), or when a boy makes a sand-castle and then destroys it with his hands and feet (xv 362–4), or when a man who after a day's ploughing goes home to supper and finds that his knees shake under him (13. 31–4), or when boys try to get a donkey out of a field of barley but break their sticks on him in the effort (xi 558–62), while he refuses to move till he has had his fill. In these little scenes there is certainly affection, even tenderness, at times pathos.

Homer's lively observation of the human scene takes in its most commonplace activities and sees something fresh in them—the fisherman who sits on a projecting rock and catches a fish with a linen line and a bronze hook (xvi 406–8); others use a net and spread the panting catch on the sand (22.384–7); a man hides a brand under ashes that he may not have to get fire from elsewhere, which is difficult for him as he lives far from neighbours (5.488–490); a cook turns a blood-pudding over a fire, and longs for it to be cooked (20.25–7); a man brings water to his plot and makes little runnels for it (xxi 257–9); dogs fawn round their master when he comes back from a feast, for they know that he has titbits for them (10.216–17); on seeing a stranger a bitch, watching over her puppies, barks and wishes to go for him (20.14–15). In such cases Homer enjoys what men and women do, but he has a special interest in some other cases which illustrate man as a craftsman. The poet who told how Odysseus made his raft, notices much in the arts and crafts of his time. A woman, from Maeonia or Caria, stains ivory with scarlet to be a cheek-piece for horses (iv 141–5); a carpenter uses a fallen poplar lying in a marsh to make a felloe for a wheel (iv 482–7); men stand in a circle and tan an ox-hide (xvii 389–93); a seated potter sends his wheel whirling round (xviii 600–1); a man bores a hole in a ship's timber with an augur, and his assistants help in turning it (9.384–6); a smith tempers an axe by dipping it in boiling water (ibid. 391–3); a metal-worker lays gold on silver (6.232–4). In a simple world Homer seems to have noticed almost everything, and we see how insecure he knew it to be. This did not lessen his love of it; on the contrary it strengthened his love of the passing scene and enabled him to record it in its many manifestations.

From this knowledge Homer was able to give strength and life to his heroic world, but there must have been much on which his tradition gave him little or no information, and in such cases he had to provide his own structure of events and their circumstances. In this he almost certainly draws on recent times. In general this was not the kind of thing that tradition would preserve in any fullness, if indeed at all, from the Mycenaean age, and what we know of that age suggests that Homer's account of social conditions is quite different. We get more information about social organization from the *Odyssey* than from the *Iliad*, and we can to some degree compare this with what we know of the Mycenaean society from its records in Linear B script. At the start it is clear that while the Mycenaean system was elaborately organized in a more or less pyramidal shape and governed by strict rules and bureaucratic regulations, there is no sign of this in Homer. A simple indication of the difference is that whereas the Mycenaean system relied extensively on records kept in documents, writing is not known to Homer, and Homeric society exists without it. We cannot be certain that Homer records precisely the social conditions of his own day; it is possible that he repeats what recent stages of tradition have brought into verse, and that these were already a little out of date. But what is certain is that his world is not Mycenaean in its social structure and that it is, unlike some of his details, consistent and convincing. If we take some main points in Homer's treatment of social conditions, we can see some underlying principles and convictions in them.

Homer in the *Iliad* certainly suggests that Agamemnon is in some sense commander-in-chief. This is clear when Odysseus, struggling to restore order among the panicking Achaeans, says:

'Not all of us Achaeans here shall be kings; many commanders is not a good thing. Let there be one commander, one king, to whom the son of crooked-hearted Cronus has given the sceptre and the dooms, that he may be king over them.' (ii 203–6)

At war Agamemnon is in command, and the sign of his command is the sceptre, which has come to him through his descent from Pelops, to whom Hermes passed it from Zeus, and is the token that he reigns 'over many islands and all Argos' (ibid. 108). This supremacy has some support in history, since the Hittite documents speak with some respect of the king of Ahhiyawa as if he were the peer of other great kings. Such no doubt he was from a military point of view, and may even have been in some sense suzerain, when Mycenae was at the height of its power. For Homer this power is clear at Troy, but limited to it. Outside his powers as commander-in-chief Agamemnon has no control of other kings or princes, each of whom has his own kingdom and his own troops. He is indeed 'most kingly' (ix 69) and has a larger contingent—100 ships—than anyone else (ii 576), but there is not the smallest hint that he has any special powers in peace or away from the united army. This may well be a reflection of Mycenaean monarchy, where perhaps the king was omnipotent in war, but only *primus inter pares*, if even that, in peace. The Linear B documents give no hint of a central monarchy, and even at Pylos the king seems to be different from the commander-in-chief. The Homeric system is much simpler, and looks as if it came from a society which, after the collapse and disintegration of a highly organized system, was struggling to reestablish order almost from the start in a much simpler and more primitive way.

The *Odyssey* deals with normal conditions in time of peace, and in it the social unit is the *oikos* or household. The household is almost a self-contained unit, with its head, his family, its free dependents, or retainers, its heralds, its slaves of both sexes. It has also its hired workers who seem not to be slaves and because they lack even the security of slaves are regarded as the most miserable of men (11.489–91). Rather different are the skilled workers, *demioergoi*, 'those who work for the people', carpenters, workers in metal, soothsayers, bards and physicians (17.383–5). These were too specialized to be fully used by one household, and seem to have served any master that summoned them. They are sent for when they are needed as is the goldsmith who gilds the horns of a bull before sacrifice (3.432 ff.). The household relies for its food on its own produce, which is brought in by slaves like Eumaeus, and consists largely of animals and not so obviously of grain. Yet though we might expect a household to be of some size, and certainly Homer suggests that it is when he allots fifty slave-women to Penelope (22.421), as he does to the fabulously rich Arete (7.103), no doubt this was much grander than in his own time and exalts his heroines. But in fact the number of slaves at Pylos seems to have been much larger than this, and the system to have been more specialized, since there are classes of slave-women who do carding, spinning, and weaving. Moreover at Pylos we find a large class of 'slavers of a god'. Whether this means a special class with special duties or whether it means they were attached to temples, of this there is no hint in Homer, where slaves belong to the master of the household. In this the Homeric system is much simpler than the Mycenaean.

In the *Iliad* the Homeric king is usually an important personage; in the *Odyssey* his power is less clearly defined. The Suitors are all princes of some kind and may be presumed to exercise power over their own domains, whether in Ithaca or elsewhere. None of these domains can have been at all large. Clearly Odysseus is in some sense suzerain, and that is why they desire his wife and position; but the nature of this is not at all clear. Kingship may in theory have been hereditary. Such no doubt it was at Mycenae, if the great bee-hive tombs come from a single dynasty. Such it may have been in most Homeric places. But heredity seems not to have been enough. We are not told why even before he went to Troy Odysseus had succeeded Laertes as king; old age was not necessarily a bar, as we see from Nestor. In his father's absence

Telemachus has some prestige but very little power, and even though he summons the assembly, anyone else had a like right to do so. Birth may have counted for something in kingship, but what really counted was personal character and power—the Homeric kings rule 'by power', which indicates authority, and is indeed the means by which Zeus keeps the gods in order.

The king is at least head of his own household and lives partly on the produce of his lands, partly on loot gained on warlike expeditions. The latter constitutes his capital. What matters is that he does not deal in trade or make money by it. In the *Odyssey* the only real trade is conducted by Phoenicians, and this is historically correct; for by the eighth century Tyre and Sidon had begun their remarkable extension of trade into the Mediterranean. They provide the Greeks with certain elegances, but they are not indispensable. Though the Phaeacians must owe something to trade, they do not value it highly and it is significant that Euryalus says discourteously to Odysseus:

'Indeed, stranger, I do not think you are like a player of games, such as there are many among men, but like one who travels with a many-benched ship, a master of trafficking sailors, who remembers his cargo and is in charge of merchandise and greedy gains.' (8.159–64)

This is grossly insulting, and Odysseus dismisses it by showing how fine an athlete he is. Trade is not part of the Homeric hero's life. But durable treasure is, and each household has its treasure-room. This is a sign of prestige, and that is why when guests depart they receive handsome gifts from their hosts, as Telemachus does from Menelaus (4.613–19) or Odysseus from Alcinous (13.10–15). In the end this system of gifts might amount to a kind of barter, as former guests became hosts in their turn and wished to display their princely generosity. This system of gifts indicates the solidarity of the ruling class. Members of it might go to war at times, but in the intervals hospitality was a first duty to strangers, and it is characteristic of the bestial Cyclops that, though he knows of his duty, he says that his guest-gift to Odysseus will be to eat him last of his company (9.369–70).

The economics of the Homeric world are much simpler than that of the Mycenaean can have been, and we may believe that in them Homer reproduced the society that he himself knew. It may have been in existence for some long time, but it clearly is not that of Mycenae, whose wares were exported to distant lands and whose social system was elaborate and clearly defined. By keeping to his own time Homer gains certain advantages. He does not have to explain how things work, and we discern in them an underlying consistency. Into this he reads his own humane interpretation of what customs mean and shows how they are. In particular the old conception of honour is just as indispensable and as central as in any truly heroic society, and provides some charming and illuminating touches on action and worth.

The Homeric characters are moved by a sense of their own worth, but they have found a peculiar way to express it. It needs success, but mere success or even the acknowledgment of it is not enough. It must be symbolized in solid form, in material objects. When the Achaean heroes compete at the funeral games of Patroclus, the victors are not content as in later days with a crown of wild olive; they expect and get solid objects of considerable worth. This is well understood by Achilles from the start:

And from his ships Achilles brought out prizes, cauldrons and tripods and horses and mules and strong oxen, and also well-girdled women and gray iron. (xxiii 259–61)

All the competitors get prizes, so that none feels himself despised or dishonoured. Antilochus, who has won a mare by cheating in the chariot-race, is chidden by Menelaus and gives the mare to him, but Menelaus in his turn gives it back. In all this the prize is the token of the man's worth and must be treated seriously. By cheating, Antilochus has behaved badly, but his apology makes amends and all is well.

Solid, visible, valuable gifts are a sign of human worth, and that is why when the Phaeacians load Odysseus with them, they do more than perform the duties of hosts to a departing guest; they stress the importance of Odysseus and their high opinion of him.

Arete the queen admires his appearance and physique and intelligence, and says that for these they must give him gifts (11.336–341). It is entirely natural and has the air of being a social custom properly applied. Odysseus has incidentally shown his athletic prowess, and deserves a reward for it, but he has done much more, and that is why there is a special call to treat him as handsomely as possible. The gifts are in this case a visible sign of his superiority to other men, which is recognized even by the somewhat complacent Phaeacians.

If goods represent honour, they have a special usefulness in making amends to anyone whose honour has been wounded. So, when Agamemnon decides that he must appease Achilles, whom he has grossly insulted, he not only offers to give back Briseis but to add a number of other handsome gifts, including twenty Trojan captives and seven cities (ix 121–56). When Achilles refuses this handsome offer, he goes too far and defies the conventions of right behaviour. The right comment is that of Aias:

'After all, even in cases of murder a man accepts blood-money for a brother or perhaps a son ... But for you, Achilles, the gods have put an implacable and evil fury in your breast because of a single girl.'
(ix 632–8)

Impalpable entities like worth and honour are equated with solid goods, and a basis is made to solve what might otherwise be insoluble problems involving personal pride.

The ransom of Hector's body by Priam from Achilles is an extension of this system. Achilles has not dishonoured Priam, but he intends to dishonour Hector by maltreating his dead body. Achilles believes that he has been wronged by Hector, who has killed Patroclus and so wounded Achilles in a very intimate place. Priam's load of treasure is meant to heal this wound; for once it is healed, Achilles will not wish to maltreat or even to keep the body of Hector. Homer understands this perfectly, but motivates the whole scene with much insight and subtlety when he makes Achilles respond to Priam not in a business deal but in pity for the old man. Yet since this is a kind of deal, and amends are made to Achilles, here, as with Agamemnon, he abates his wrath and brings a chapter to an end. The Homeric Greeks live much less for abstractions than for actual objects of value. Through their acquisition of these, they have a more solid testimony to their worth.

This system applies only to the noble, the god-born, the god-like, the kings and princes. Within their own society of equals, they stand normally by one another. This does not prevent them from conducting raids and feuds at the expense of their neighbours, but outside these there are certain obligations which a society follows because it is not very sure of itself. Though Homer says next to nothing about the ordinary people, and though in the world which he knew they must have been kept in some sort of order, it looks as if the princely class regarded its own solidarity as more important than any obligations to its social inferiors. This explains why unknown and unexpected guests are treated with courtesy and generosity, not even being asked their names until they have been washed and fed. It explains also the remarkable way in which fugitives from justice are given asylum. Justice is the affair not of the state but of the family, and any fugitive from it may claim help from some other family. So Phoenix is persuaded by his mother to sleep with his father's concubine. His father lays a solemn curse on him, and he leaves his home, but finds safety and honour with Peleus, where he looks after the young Achilles (ix 447–91). His crime concerns only his father and family, and he has a fine chance to start a new career. As a boy Patroclus killed the son of Amphidamas and was given a home by Peleus (xxiii 85–90). Theoclymenus has killed a man in his own clan and flees from the vengeance of his many kinsmen. He does not attempt to justify himself when he seeks protection from Telemachus, who takes him, without enquiry, on his ship (15.256–81). This is clearly the right thing to do, and Telemachus may be presumed to see that Theoclymenus is a member of his own class, a man with whom it is proper to have formal relations without asking questions. He does not even ask his name; still less is there any hint that a murderer may be polluted and bring harm to those who harbour him. On this point Homeric opinion and custom are remarkably realistic and clear-headed.

The head of a household may of course be a king and rule over subjects, who are free men like himself but over whom he exerts authority partly by some hereditary claim, partly by superiority of gifts and talents and character. But his rôle is essentially paternal. Since there is no writing, there are no written laws for him to keep and apply. The best he can do is to act according to tradition, in accord with the *themistes* or 'dooms' which belong to him as king (i 238; ii 206; ix 99), and which he interprets for himself. The good king takes care of his people. So Telemachus says that his father was 'gentle as a father' (2.47), and the same words are used of him by Athene (5.12). Though heroes are, with the exception of the Asiatic Priam, monogamous, there is nothing against their taking concubines, as Agamemnon takes Chryseis or Odysseus lives with Circe and Calypso, or Menelaus has a son by a slave in the absence of Helen (4.12). But practice was not always so tolerant as theory. The mother of Phoenix objected violently when she was supplanted by a rival (ix 451), and Laertes prudently abstained from sleeping with the young Eurycleia because he was afraid of his wife's anger (1.433). The Homeric hero is bound by strong notions of *noblesse oblige* but they are not always the same as those of modern times.

This social system which is clearly presupposed in the *Odyssey* and is not absent from the *Iliad* must have been that which prevailed in Greece between the collapse of the Mycenaean world and the growth of the city-state. No doubt it was in full function in the ninth and eighth centuries, but began to dissolve about 700. Homer knows it and makes use of it for his story. The importance of the household as the centre of social organization, wealth and power explains much in the *Odyssey*. Odysseus, who rules by virtue of descent and great personal superiority, is away, and the question arises of who should take his place. In the meanwhile nobody quite knows what is the thing to do, and just because neither Penelope nor Telemachus can exert full control, there is real danger of a disaster in which one of the Suitors will acquire power. Odysseus is right to kill them, not only because they devour his substance and seek to marry his wife, but because they wish to lay hands on his household, and this is the centre of his life and position. He cannot possibly allow it, and therefore he kills them. Moreover, because vengeance belongs to the household the families of the dead Suitors are obliged to seek recompense for their death. In the scene in 24.422 ff. when Eupeithes, son of Antinous, urges others to take vengeance, it is clear that this is their duty as kinsmen of the dead, and they will be held in lasting dishonour if they shirk their task. They in fact attempt it, but are foiled by Athene and Odysseus, though the defeat is not final and is left as a source of uneasiness at the end of the poem. Homer understands this kind of society from the inside and, though tradition may well have helped him in many ways with it, he did not necessarily need it.

In one respect Homer indicates a contradiction between his heroic characters and the outlook which he knew. We have seen that a man's life could be valued, and if the right price was paid, there was no more need for vengeance. On the Shield of Achilles he describes an arbitration about the fee for a man killed. It is conducted before elders and two talents of gold are at stake, but the dispute continues about the actual amount (xviii 497–508). This seems to be normal and its presence in a simile, in which the judges are not a king but elders, suggests that it is Homer's own time. But this assessment of a man's life in terms of gold or oxen or some other valuable property does not apply to the heroic temper when it gets to work. For instance, in war prisoners may be ransomed, and the young Trojan prince Lycaon is ransomed for a large sum (xxi 42) and brought back to Troy, where, after eleven days with his friends, he is caught unarmed by Achilles, and this time the heroic spirit of Achilles allows no talk of mercy (ibid. 99 ff.). A similar aversion to equation is in Achilles' mind when, in his first refusal of the amends of Agamemnon, he says:

'Oxen and strong flocks can be looted, and tripods and the yellow heads of horses can be bought, but the life of a man can be neither looted nor bought once it has passed the barrier of his teeth.' (ix 406–9)

This is the heroic spirit in full reverse. Achilles turns for the moment against his usual outlook and states its opposite, but in denying it with this emphasis he shows how much it means to him, how deeply it is engrained in his nature. His normal view is that a man's life is not so important as his honour, and must in the last resort be sacrificed to it, as he knows that his own will be (xxi 110–13). The hero knows that he will be killed sooner or later, and when he has to choose between caution and danger, chooses danger. Hector derides Polydamas when he counsels withdrawal (xii 210), and though he takes his advice in letting the Trojans retire into the city (xviii 249), does not do so himself. When there is a conflict between prudence and honour, honour wins. Priam and Hecuba both beg Hector not to fight Achilles because they know that he will be killed (xxii 25 ff.), but Hector, who knows that this is true, follows honour to death. He even knows that it is the ruin of his own people whom he destroys by his insistence on fighting (xxii 107). He makes up his mind:

'Then it would be far better for me to face Achilles and either to kill him and return home or myself to be killed gloriously before the city.'
(xxii 108–10)

This sacrifice of life to honour is central to the heroic outlook and contradicts its otherwise business-like assessment of a human life in terms of oxen.

There is nothing surprising in the Homeric combination of the heroic ideal, with its strong demand for honour, and an everyday outlook on many social matters. Such a contrast has always existed in societies which are in any way concerned with war; for without some heroic picture of himself the soldier would miss the impulse to exert himself to the utmost. In Homer's own world such an ideal would be natural, perhaps even common. That he himself knew about war is clear from the city at war on the Shield (xviii 509–40), and though we know very little of the political events of the eighth century we can hardly doubt that war played a large part in them, as when exiles from Colophon seized Smyrna (Herodotus 1.150) or troops from Chios captured Erythrae

(Hippias of Erythrae, 421 F 1 Jacoby). In the seventh century Archilochus of Paros spent a large part of his time in various campaigns in the island of Thasos and on the Thracian mainland, but seems to have had no illusions that he was a hero, though no doubt some of his contemporaries thought that they were. Where Homer's world differed from the world of legend and tradition was not in the degree of its belief in heroism, but in the sad fact that its wars were small and local and not comparable with the huge Panhellenic effort against Troy. Homer transfers what he must himself have seen on a small scale to events on a large scale, and thus keeps them alive and impressive. No doubt his sense of heroic values helped him to ennoble familiar traits and actions, but they remain within the bounds of a convincing actuality. We do not notice anachronisms or archaisms in this sphere, for they do not exist as such.

Homer may conceivably have made some slight confusion between kingship as he knew about it from tradition and as he saw it at work in his own day. The great chieftains at Troy have their own quite extensive domains, and bring suitable contingents. Whatever historical truth there is in these figures, at least in the story they suggest commanders with forces worth commanding. Agamemnon brings a hundred ships (ii 576), and this is meant to impress. The grand alliance of the Achaeans in the *Iliad* is based on legend, and is very unlikely to have anything corresponding to it in the poet's own day. We suspect, with some reason, that what he knew was a system of many small princes, perhaps owing some allegiance here and there to an overlord, but for most purposes managing their own small domains. Such are the Suitors, who come from the western islands and have no large property in land. Elsewhere, perhaps, Nestor and Menelaus rule substantial kingdoms, but they belong to legend and have no part in the world of the Suitors. The Suitors are called 'kings' (1.394; 18.64; 20.196), and no doubt this reflects current practice; the title and no doubt the task have come down in the world, and we are tempted to suspect that in Homer's times kings were very much what they were for Hesiod. Hesiod has no love for them, but refers only to their injustice in giving verdicts (*Works and Days* 37–41) and warns them that the gods will punish them for their misdoings (ibid. 249 ff.). But these kings seem to be judges and no more, and it looks as if monarchy in its decline had lost its power to rule but kept its juridical powers, which it exercised badly. If so, Hesiod represents a political stage later than Homer's, not indeed much later but sufficiently so for the word 'king' to convey a different meaning. Both are far removed from any great kings of the Achaeans who were addressed as equals by the kings of the Hittites.

In the *Odyssey* the household is the unit of order and organization. The palace of Odysseus is situated in what is called a city, but seems to be the only one on Ithaca. In it some of the Suitors live in their own houses. But though there is a city, and it stands by a harbour, it is not a city in the same sense as Troy. In so far as the inhabitants feel any solidarity it is as Ithacans (2.25, 161, 229; 24.454), and their city plays no part. This must have been the case in many parts of Greece when the unit of habitation was the single farm in the countryside, and it was from the union of farms and hamlets that villages came. This was the view of Thucydides (1.2). Homer presents two different systems, on the one hand large cities with well developed characteristics, on the other a motley collection of households. Both may have existed simultaneously, and the second survived because it had less chance of development. But the historical process was from villages to cities. In Attica this came when Theseus united the villages and put them under a single government. In the *Odyssey* Odysseus might have done this.

Bibliographical Note

THE author of this book probably intended to give some information about books on Homer which might be useful to the reader; here, then are some remarks about such books.

Bowra's own *Heroic Poetry* (London, 1952) gives a learned, and also readable, account of the epic poems which may most suitably be compared with Homer's.

G. S. Kirk's *The Songs of Homer* (Cambridge, 1962) gives the best general account of the problems presented by the Homeric poems.

The Language and Background of Homer, edited by G. S. Kirk (Cambridge, 1964), contains thirteen of the more interesting articles about Homer published during the ten years before its appearance. All except one are in English, and several are not too difficult for the general reader.

The first two chapters of *The Justice of Zeus* by Hugh Lloyd-Jones (Berkeley and Los Angeles, 1971) discuss problems of Homeric ethics and religion.

Denys L. Page's *History and the Homeric Iliad* (Berkeley and Los Angeles, 1959) is an extremely well-written study of the historical background to the Homeric poems, making use of modern evidence from archaeological data and from Oriental documents. Page is somewhat optimistic about the amount of actual history reflected in the epics; for a more pessimistic view, see M. I. Finley in *Journal of Hellenic Studies* 84, 1964, 1f. (followed by replies from Kirk, Page and J. L. Caskey).

The Making of Homeric Verse (Oxford, 1971) contains the collected papers of Milman Parry, whose immense contribution to Homeric studies is discussed by Bowra in this book, especially in the second chapter. The volume has been edited and the works written in French translated by Milman Parry's son, Adam Milman Parry, who died in a road accident on 4 June, 1971. Adam Parry's introduction to the volume is the best short account of the present state of the Homeric Question now available, at least in English.

H. Ll.-J.

Index

References in italic type relate to the illustrations, identified by numbers.

Abdul Hamid, *11*, 21

Achaeans, 10, 20, 21, 34, 36–9, 45, 47, 55–9, 63–73, 78, 82, 83–5, 88–92, 96–116, 153, 156, 158, 172, 175, 182

Achilles, 10, 34–44, 48, 49, 50, 54–9, 64, 67–73, 77, 88, 100, 110, 117, 121, 122, 142, 144, 149, 150, 155, 157, 161, 167, *28, 29, 32*; epithets of, 14, 19, 23, 24; characterization of, 99, 108, 113–16, 158, 159, 175, 176, 179–80; Mycenean origin of, 83, 87; quarrel with Agamemnon, 110, 113, 154, 155; shield of, 51, 147–8, 168, 179; similes, 63, 65; wrath of, 6, 39, 49, 69, 97–8, 104–6, 177

Achins of Sumatra, 12

Adamas, 43

Aegisthus, 23, 137

Aegyptus, 56

Aeneas, 57, 67–8, 109, 133

Aeneid, 2

Aeolus, 71, 76, 133

Agamemnon, 24, 34, 42, 50, 52, 55, 56, 58, 69, 70, 85, 90, 91, 92, 100, 101, 108, 116, 120, 121, 122, 137; epithets of, 19, 33; quarrel with Achilles, 36–7, 39, 43, 77, 98–9, 106, 110, 113; similes, 62, 65

Aias, 39, 46, 47, 54, 59, 63, 70, 71, 92, 102, 114, 121, 122

Ainu of Hokkaido, 12 (and see *Kulune Shirka*)

Alaman Bet, 76

Albania, 12

Alcinous, 10, 11, 87, 93, 136, 139, 144, 145, 152, 164, 174

Alexander, 83, 86

Alexandria, 7

Alphesiboia, 50

Amenhotep III, 88

Amphidamas, 177

Amphimedon, 130

Amphinomus, 136

anachronism, 10, 17–18, 24–5, 39–41, 46–53, 89–96, 146

Anatolia, 82

Andromache, 36, 45, 57, 69, 107, 113, 116, 157, 158–9

Antenor, 56

Anticlea, 47, 55, 160

Antilochus, 122, 158, 175

Antinous, 57, 78, 136

Antiphus, 70

Aphrodite, 13, 22, 23, 50, 70, 101, 109–11, 133, 137, 153, 161, 162

Apollo, 14, 16, 22, 23, 37, 55, 60, 69, 104, 105, 109, 110

Arcadia, 22, 26, 27; dialect of, 22

Archilochus, 54, 181

Ares, 13, 20, 35, 62, 109, 111, 137, 153

Arete, 59, 173, 176

Argives, 20
Argos, 20, 57, 88–9, 90, 91, 172
Argos (Odysseus' dog), 72, 129, 157
Ariosto, 32
Arisbe, 56
Aristarchus, 54, 58, 131
aristeia, 67
Aristophanes, 131
Aristotle, 50
arms and armour, 46–7, 51, 87–8, *6, 12, 13, 14, 15, 16, 17*
Asia, 1, 12, 26, 48, 83, 93, 168
Asine, 49
Asius, 17
Assurbanipal, 166
Asteris, 152
Astyanax, 157
Athene, 14, 18, 22, 33–5, 44, 55, 74, 75, 97, 109, 110, 128, 133, 137, 153
Athens, 2, 84, 92
Atreus, 114
Attica, 48, 182
Attila, 80, 85
Aubignac, Abbé d', see Hédelin
Aulis, 89, 91
Axylus, 56

Basques, 80
Bellerophon, 12, 68, 77
Beowulf, 3, 28, 80, 153
Boeotians, 89, 91
Boghaz-Köy, 82
bride-price, and dowry, 49–51
Briseis, 39, 44, 98, 107, 176, *26*
Bulgaria, 12
burial, 47–9

Cadmus, 79
Calypso, 36, 55, 61, 71, 74, 77, 118, 121, 124, 127, 135, 144, 147, 160, 168, 178
Camoens, 2

Cape Helles, 81
Carians, 20, 93
Carthage, 44
Cassandra, 49, 56
Catalogue of Achaean ships, 89–92, 100
Catalogue of Trojan allies, 92–3, 100
Cefalonia, 152
Cebriones, 63
Charlemagne, 80
Charybdis, 71
Chimaera, 68, 134
Chios, 115, 180
Chryseis, 154, 178
Chryses, 43, 55
Ciconians, 143
Circe, 23, 71, 72, 77, 121, 126–8, 133, 145, 168, 178
Clytaemnestra, 122, 132
Colophon, 180
Corinth, 90, 91
cremation, 48–9, 51
Crete, 52, 81, 82, 91, 94
Cronus, 58, 68
Cypria, 97
Cyclops, 23, 39–40, 56, 64, 66, 71, 72, 117, 121, 125, 133, 162, 174, *9, 10, 11*
Cyprus, 26, 49, 87

Danaans, 2
Dardanians, 20
Dark Age, 51–2
David of Sassoun, 5
Deiphobus, 110
Delphi, 52
Demodocus, 10, 11, 13, 15, 111, 137, 153, 163, 165, 166
Dendra, 49
Diogenes Laertius, 92
Diomedes, 34–5, 54–5, 63, 65, 68, 74, 77, 85, 101, 109, 153, 154

Dodona, 22
Dolon, 54, 113, 121, 156
Dorian invasion, 20, 27, 52, 84, 91
dowry, see bride-price

Egypt, 51, 52, 78
Elder Edda, 3, 13, 28, 85, 153, 166, 167
Elpenor, 48, 56
embalming, 48
Enkidu, 59
Enkomi, 49
Ephyra, 56
epithets, 18–24 (see also under individual heroes)
Ermanaric, 80
Erythrae, 180
Esthonian poetry, see *Kalewipoeg*
Eumaeus, 55, 65, 75, 77–8, 118, 129, 136, 145, 154, 166, 173
Eumelus, 59
Euryalus, 56, 136, 174
Euryclea, 35, 129, 134, 136
Eurylochus, 77
Eurymachus, 50, 131, 136
Eurypylus, 103

formulae, 13–30, 32–3, 40, 42, 44, 46, 51, 95–6
funeral rites, 47–9, 51

Gargarus, 111
Gilgamesh, 3, 13, 28, 59, 60, 76, 108, 109, 128, 139, 141, 153, 166
Glaucus, 38, 44, 55, 68, 74, 77, 83, 87, 112, 153, 158
Gorgythion, 63

Hadibrand, 67
Halitherses, 58
Harpalion, 63
Hattusas, 82
Hecamede, 70

Hector, 34, 40–2, 45, 48, 55–8, 69, 83, 104, 106–16, 146, 148–51, 154, 156–63, 180, 27, 29; death of, 40, 48, 73, 114, 149, 176; heroism of, 36, 70–1, 102, 113; humanity of, 108, 115, 157, 159; marriage of, 49; similes, 65, 66
Hecuba, 159, 180
Hédelin, F.
Helen, 24, 55, 70, 79, 88, 99, 107, 114, 123, 156, 162, 163, 178
Hephaestus, 23, 50, 52, 87, 144, 145, 147
Hera, 16, 22, 34, 44, 57, 58, 69, 73, 97, 103, 110, 111, 133, 146, 161, 162
Hesiod, 11, 79, 85, 142, 166, 167, 181–2
hexameter, 15, 45, 94–6
Hildebrand, 67
Hisarlik, 21, 81
Hittites, 51, 82–3, 88, 172, 182
Hoplite, *17*

Ida, 22
Idomeneus, 54, 56
ikhōr, 111
Iliad, 117–21, 134–8, 166, 171, 173, 178; anachronisms in narrative of, 46–53; as poetry of action, 141–64; as epic poetry, 2–3; as oral heroic poetry, 12–13; as product of Greek Heroic Age, 79–96; poems contemporary with, 2; criticism of, 3–9; devices of composition in, 54–78; epithets in, 18–24; inconsistencies of narrative in, 32–45; Milman Parry's theory of formulae in, 13–30; oral composition of, 10–31, 46–53; origins of, 1–2, 30, 38; shape and character of, 97–116

Ilium, 44, 45
Indian epics, see *Mahābhārata* and *Ramayana*
In-tepe Asmak (Simois?), 150
Iolcus, 90
Iphidamas, 56
Iphition, 54
Iris, 110, 155
Irus, 23, 35, 136, 143
Ischia, 2
Ishtar, 61
Ismarus, 71
Isos, 70
Ithaca, 2, 10, 23, 33, 57, 72, 74–6, 119, 131, 132, 135–7, 145, 151, 152, 173, 182, *39*
Itylus, 62

Jugoslav poetry, 12, 24–6, 59, 60

Kadesh, 51
Kalevala, 4–5
Kalewipoeg, 5
Kalka, battle of, 80
Kalmucks, 60
Karalaev, Saiakbai, 26
Keftiu, 94
Keteioi, 88
Kirghiz, 60, 61, 76
Knossos, 83
Kosovo, battle of, 80, 85
Kreutzwald, F. R., 5
Kulune Shirka, 76

Lacedaemon, 21, 24
Lachmann, K. 4–1
Laertes, 129, 130, 132, 173, 178
Laestrygonians, 71–2, 145
Lampetie, 77
Laodamus, 136
Laomedon, 108, 162
Laothoe, 50

Lemnos, 89
Leucas, 152
Linear B script, 94, 171, 2, 3
'Longinus', 119, 139
Lönnrot, E. 4–5
Lotus-eaters, 71, 72
Lusiads, 2
Lycaon, 112, 179
Lycia, 20, 68

Mahābhārata, 5
Malays of Borneo, 12
Maldon, 3, 116
Manas, 26, 76, 141
Maoris, 80, 90
Marko, 59
Megara, 91
Meges, 56, 90
Meleager, 39, 77
Melantho, 136
Melanthus, 136
Menander, 119
Mendere (Scamander?), 150
Menelaus, 32, 48, 54–8, 87, 88, 91, 120, 123, 156, 174, 175, 178; duel with Paris, 58, 70, 71, 99, 100–1, 106, 109, 162; similes, 61; wealth of, 145, 181
Menesthius, 56
Mentes, 33
Miletus, 93
Milton, 2
Minoan culture, 46, 81–2
Minos, 81, 139
Mongols, 12, 80, 85, 86, 153
Monomakh, V., 80
Muses, 30, 89, 97, 117
Mycenae, 63; culture of, 27, 31, 60, 46–52, 82–96, 146, 171–3, 175, 178; language of, 27, 83, 171; metalwork of, 87, 148, *8*, *19*, *20*, *23*, *25*; poetry of, 94–6

Myrmidons, 56, 102, 103, 105, 107, 161

Nausicaa, 17, 41, 75, 124, 125, 167
Neoptolemus, 88, 121
Nestor, 19, 51, 70, 101, 103, 120, 145, 173, 181; cup of, 51, *20*; palace of, *37, 38*
Nibelungenlied, 4, 6
Noah, 76
Norsemen, 80

Odysseus, 15, 17, 39–41, 43, 46–7, 48, 52, 55, 57, 58, 59, 64, 65, 71–8, 92, 93, 100, 102, 114, 117–40, 142, 144–7, 152, 155, 157, 162, 167–70, 172, *36*; characterization of, 34–6, 159–60, 173–6, 178, 179, 182; epithets of, 16, 19, 23
Odyssey, 111, 114, 171, 173, 174, 182; anachronisms in narrative of, 46–53; as poetry of action, 141–64; as epic poetry, 2–3; as oral heroic poetry, 12–13; as product of Greek Heroic Age, 79–96; poems contemporary with, 2; criticism of, 3–9; devices of composition in, 54–78; epithets of, 18–24; Inconsistencies in narrative of, 32–45; Milman Parry's theory of formulae in, 13–30; oral composition of, 10–31, 46–53; origins of, 1–2, 30, 39; shape and character of, 117–40
Ogygia, 65
Oïleus, 47
Old Testament, 5
Olympus, 22, 57, 69, 74, 111, 137, 140
oral composition, 10–31; problems of, 46–53
Orestes, 114

Orion, 139, 140
Orlando Furioso, 32
Orozbakoc, Saghimbai, 26
Othryoneus, 49, 54, 56

Pandareos, 62
Pandarus, 54, 83, 110, 114, 146
Paphlagonians, 32
Paradise Lost, 2
Paris, 83, 114; abduction of Helen; 70, 120, 163; duel with Menelaus, 55, 57, 58, 71, 99, 100–1, 133, Judgment of, 97, 108, 162; similes, 42, 65
Parry, M., 13n, 13–15, 24, 28
Patroclus, 22, 37, 58, 63, 69, 103–13, 122, 142, 150, 154, 158, 161, *28*; death of, 24, 38, 40, 57, 65, 66, 70, 104–13, 148, 159; funeral of, 48, 49, 56, 73, 149, 175
Pedaeus, 56
Peleus, 56, 90, 97, 159, 177
Pelion, 90
Peloponnese, 20, 27, 89
Penelope, 10, 41, 50, 51, 55, 57, 72, 125, 129–32, 145, 163, 173, 178, *35*; epithets of, 19, 62; character of, 121, 135–6, 159–60
Penthesilea, 167
Phaeacia, 10, 56, 57, 59, 65, 71, 75, 87, 117, 124, 137, 144, 145, 174, 175
Phemius, 10, 11, 163, 165, 166
Phereboia, 50
Polydamas, 112, 180
Polyphemus, see Cyclops
Polypoetes, 66
Poseidon, 22, 34, 62, 69, 108, 110, 137, 162
Priam, 24, 40, 43, 45, 56, 57, 70, 142, 159, 180; and Helen, 100, 101, 107, 120; marriage of, 50, 78; ransoms

Priam—*cont.*
   Hector's body, 64, 73, 105–6, 113,
      146, 151, 176, *32*; similes, 64
Protesilaos, 89
Pylaemenes, 32–3
Pylos, 21, 75, 81, 83, 84, 93, 95, 120,
      131, 135, 172, 173, *37, 38*

Quintilian, 92

Racine, 135
Radermacher, L., 124
Radlov, 28
Ramadan, 59
Ramayana, 5
Rameses, 114
Ras Shamra, 90
Rhapsode, *5*
Rhodes, 88, 91
Rome, 44
Russia, 12, 80
Rustum, 67

sacrifice, human and animal, 17, 49, *8*
Salamis, 49, 92, *8*
Saracens, 80
Sarpedon, 17, 38, 48, 66, 104, 109,
      112, 154, 158, 161
Scamander, 23, 104, 109, 144, 150
Schliemann, H. 48, 81
Scipio Africanus, 44
Scylla, 71, 133–4, *33*
Seneca, 7
Serbs, 80
Sidon, 174
Sicyon, 90
Sigarth, 114
Similes, 60–6 (see also under indi-
      vidual heroes)
Simois, 150
Sirens, 133
Sisyphus, 139

Smyrna, 84, 180
Song of Roland, 3, 13, 80, 85, 116, 153
Sparta, 75, 91, 120, 123, 145
Sthenelus, 54
Strabo, 92
Suitors, 6, 11, 69–70, 72, 75, 118–19,
      122–3, 130, 131, 132, 135, 136, 182

Tahiti, 90
Tantalus, 139
Tatars, 25, 86, 153
Taygetus, 21
Telemachus, 10, 35, 50, 55, 58, 65,
      71–5, 87, 118, 123, 131, 134, 135,
      142, 174, 177–8, *35*
Terpiades, 163
Thasos, 181
Theano, 56
Thebaid, 85
Thebes, 21, 79, 88
Theoclymenus, 58, 72, 131, 177
Theodoric, 80
Thersites, 113, 121, 136, 143, 153, 156
Theseus, 182
Thessaly, 90, 91
Thetis, 23, 43, 97, 99, 106–9, 159
Thrace, 56
Thrinacia, 128
Thucydides, 91, 182
Tiresias, 127–8
Tiryns, 21, 81, *22*
Tithonus, 16
Tityus, 139
Tmolus, 56
Trojan allies, see Catalogue of
Trojan War, 90, 91, 97, 98–116, 119
Trojans, 20, 21, 34–8, 42, 45, 47, 51,
      57, 58, 65, 66, 67, 79–96, 97–116,
      149
Troy, 10, 19, 24, 36, 48, 55–8, 70, 98,
      123, 129, 137, 138, 162, 173;
      destruction of, 45, 83, 85, 105, 117,

159, 163; epithets of, 21, 145, 151; excavations at, 81; siege of, 79, 86; similes, 64; site of, 81, 82, 85, 149, 150; tales of, 71, 115; walls of, 7, 21

Turks, 12, 25, 80

Tyre, 174

Uganda, 90,
Uta-Napishtim, 76, 128, 139

Vaphio cups, 87, *24*
Vathy, 145, 152

Virgil, 2, 153

Wade-Gery, H. T., 13n.
Welsh, 80
Wilamowitz-Moellendorf, U. von, 6
Wolf, F. A., 4
Wooden Horse, 11, 15
writing, 12, 52, 83, 94–6, 171

Zeus, 14, 16, 22, 34, 43, 44, 55, 58, 62, 63, 68, 73, 76, 79, 97, 99, 103, 104, 106, 109, 110–11, 117, 137 146, 161, 164, 167, 174

Acknowledgments

The publishers gratefully acknowledge permission to reproduce photographs from the following sources:

Alphabet and Image, 39; Professor C. W. Blegen, 7, 21, 37, 38; British Museum, by courtesy of the Trustees, 5, 30; British Museum (photo Ray Gardiner) 33; Peter Clayton, 22; Ecole Française d'Athènes, 14, 17; Heraklion Museum (photo Peter Clayton) 13; Professor Max Hirmer, 9, 12, 20, 25, 26; Dr Vassos Karagheorghis, 8; Kunsthistorische Museen, Vienna, 6, 31, 32; Mansell Collection, 2, 3, 10, 11, 16, 18, 29, 34, 35, 36; Martin von Wagner Museum, Wurzburg, 27; National Museum Athens, 4 (photo Peter Clayton) 15, 23; Josephine Powell, 19, 24; Staatliche Museen, Berlin, 1, 28.